The Tao of the Dow

Economics of Being

By Nelson Abreu, BSEE, PE, MS

With the support of:

Copyright © 2020 Nelson Abreu

Cover Art by Daniel Fausto

All rights reserved. This book or any portion thereof may not be reproduced or used in any manner whatsoever without the express written permission of the publisher except for the use of brief quotations in a book review.

First Printing, April 22, 2020 (Earth Day)

Consciousness Publishing
L.N.F@icloud.com

Dedication

I dedicate this book to the quiet heroes who, each day, contribute to the health, safety, happiness and development of their fellow humans.

Acknowledgements

This book would not be possible without the mentorship and inspiration I benefited from various fronts, including non-profit organizations IAC, ICRL, IANDS, and SSE.

Special thanks to Manori Sumanasinghe, Paulo Vieira de Castro, Mohammadreza Bashiri, Farid Khavari, Alfredo Cunhal Sendim, Victor Mendes, and Mark Anielski for rich conversations on conscious leadership, work and economics and their contributions to this work. Thank you to the talented graphic designer Daniel Fausto for the cover art. Finally, thank you to my editor for pulling all of this together, including assisting with time-consuming transcriptions.

Nelson Abreu

Foreword
Paulo Vieira de Castro

Toward an Economy of Care, Stewardship and Radical Commitment

The times require a radical commitment. For us this means that the economy can never be separated from the environment, climate, and well-being of all beings. Based on this conviction, it becomes easy to see that, especially today, there are very few economic decisions that, even from a strictly technical point of view, can be divorced from other considerations. Most of them will have to first be sustainable, ethical and moral so we do not continue to find ourselves in an unprecedented planetary crisis.

Let us start with a concrete example to approach this new commitment regarding the economy. In 2015, the world made a decision: to reduce greenhouse gas emissions in order to control global warming below 2 °C in a context of sustainable development. However, until the world is able to resolve this issue, reaching the goal agreed in Paris, all other efforts are not enough. If this obligation of participation by all nations - and not just rich countries - in the fight against environmental and climatic changes is not fulfilled, we will be facing the contours of a huge planetary emergency.

If there is, as is believed, a relationship between GDP growth and emissions of some gases, especially CO_2, then we should not understand the economy through the exclusive bias of economic growth, especially when it means growth at any price provided by indicators such as GDP. Now is the time for change, especially when it is estimated that we are on the way to a new radical compromise, and consequently, a new economic reality.

Asking the right questions

The Tao of the Dow

I return to a question I first asked in 2006. Are you more concerned with the end of the month or the end of the world? It becomes evident that it is useless to be frightened by the end of the month if there is no world. This is the risk we are currently taking, i.e. seeing the tree but ignoring the forest. And that's where we have to start. In the face of climate and environmental catastrophe, it is urgent to change the economic and financial models that have brought us here. These are certainly not the economic models that will get us out of here. They just brought us here. The economy, the environment and the climate cannot be separated.

In this way, the emergence of a new ministry or department is founded: The Ministry of Environment, Climate and Economic Relations [1]. The pillars of this new economy will be the environment, the climate and well-being [2] of all beings through the development of the empathic society, in other words, the launching of the commitment and radical responsibility of the human being towards the planet. This includes everyone, assuming that the ministry of economics would be under the responsibility of a ministry for environmental and climate issues. The times are, therefore, of responsibility and radical commitment.

The modern economic schism and the end of democracy

The economy as we know it at the moment is in a space of global anguish, as it does not integrate the (free) mind. I insist that this is where the contemporary economic crisis is founded. This is the result of the most fratricidal of all wars: the struggle, at any cost, for the mental control of the human being.

Social networks, once seen as the solution to a new economy, have also created setbacks. This solution has become the problem. Parliamentary democracy is now threatened by social networks. The priorities are created from the base of the pyramid, thus allowing new populisms. The masses represent themselves through social networks, dispensing with the mediation of the media and the

Foreword

politicians elected by them. The result could not be worse for democracy. Or what's left of it.

This reality causes the exponential growth of uncontrollable factors in the modern economy, through a globalization of democratized access to the media, proving to be uncomfortable, essentially, on the supply side. Everything became too uncertain. As a way of countering these challenges, the economy has taken on a new doctrine, now approaching any religion, thereby indoctrinating, not informing anymore.

What do economics, business and religion have in common?

The economy, business, as well as all religions, are now hostage to a common word: secrecy. They now depend on secret codes, some transformed into magical algorithms, sharing the same human mind control strategy. In other words, committed to the myth of progress, religion and economics started to have as their main objective reaching the human mind. This became the object of attention of business activity. At the same pace as religion, spirituality and some therapies are becoming commercialized, even competing amongst themselves in many aspects.

But the main reason why all of them fail is that the mind is not quiet in itself. The mind is not a fixed point in space, so fear appears as the main means of mental control.

Economics pseudoscience, why?

Because it has become averse to evaluation, especially by specialists/technicians from other areas, as if wanting to go on its own, ceasing to be rigorous when it comes to intention. Due to the obsession with the objectives of only a few, we see the multiple regulators of the economy not exercising the reason why they exist. As a bigger example than I just said, we can mention the case of central banks, unable to detect the subprime crisis, for example. In addition to regulation, there as a lack of clarity and systematization.

The Tao of the Dow

For all these reasons, one should, in my opinion, question its status as a social science. It should be noted that the validity of most of its analysis and information support tools, especially those based on statistical processes, will not be affected by my statement.

The great challenge lies in a new moral conceptualization of the economy, a new awareness. Only in this way can we meet the challenge that was at its origin as a science.

You can't make a different world with people indifferent to the idea of a better place for everyone. You cannot grow infinitely in the face of an economy based on the finite resources of a devastated planet in favor of so few.

As long as we don't change the words that will move us forward, the world will continue to be a place for just a few. In economics this will mean, for example, replacing the word growth with the much-forgotten word caring. They are, therefore, simple things that I propose. It is nothing complicated. Nor does it depend on a large financial budget.

The idea of humans being slaves to economic models has proved to be flawed, justifying itself that today, at this very moment, there are people on the street willing to die in defense of the obvious. And what world is this in which to be fair you have to be crazy?

The economics of care

The human enterprise will have to abandon the ideal of growth in order to mature and find, finally, a broader meaning for what it thinks or does.

This idea applies to everything that is the realization of man, so also the economy, politics, religion, business will have to undertake such a transformation. Likewise, countries' wealth should not be measured by GDP, but through what I call the Integral Peoples' Well-Being (BIP). Only then will we ensure that this wealth reaches everyone.

Foreword

I often meet people who tell me they are waiting for a sign, something to tell them where, why or how to change. Nowadays, change, transformation without effort, has become the most attractive business along with fear. In the face of this unease, I usually reply: you are wrong! Conscience, God if you want, is waiting for your sign. That's why it set you free, that's why it gave you total freedom to choose your own path. And this applies to organizations, people, teams, etc.

The human enterprise

Revolutions do not happen due to hunger or misery, they are always the result of a new conscience. Fear, suffering, pain, ego, are forces that contaminate our reality, preventing us from expressing self-awareness in everything we do. This is, without a doubt, the greatest of all crises!
This change in the world is an effort that does not depend on war strategies, much less on any puzzle, nor on the financial markets, just on refocusing on this idea of caring. The Economics of Caring is opposed to the Economics of Fear.
I remember that the present crisis, especially the economic one, is more than any other thing, the result of our lack of love. As in life, in economics we should also focus primarily on caring for the soul of relationships. That alone would be enough to resolve all wars, all hatred.
Caring has become the most overlooked word in the competitive world of companies, schools and, perhaps because of that, of our lives. When introducing care in the context of business and economics, we begin to perceive all relationships from the point of view of the quantum paradigm, taking into account the ability of more subtle levels of human (natural) experience to interfere (interdependent) in the creation of new multidimensional realities. Only then will we increase the real, authentic proximity between all beings on the planet.

The Tao of the Dow

Also in companies, schools, families, caring means being able to exist, having hope again, promoting conditions of reciprocity, cooperation and full acceptance. This transformation will be a distinctive element in the construction of a new way of seeing the world based on new questions.

The ethics of care

To change we must, before anything, be aware. A world without focus can never be sustainable. My children already belong to an unfocused generation. They lost the center, the ability to pay attention and, with that, the opportunity to love.

A world without focus is a world without attention. Simone Weil taught us that to love is to be attentive. In order to know who you love, it is enough to ask yourself what you are watching for, so Saint Augustine challenged us. Loving and attentive presence are qualities that are increasingly necessary to ethics, especially in the face of issues such as the sustainability of the planet and consequently of the economy. Attention is likewise the mother of all virtues. There is no weapon more effective than attention. If you give, you receive.
Being a caregiver, healer, brother, citizen...it only depends on attention. Why would the economy stay out of this dimension of human responsibility? If you don't love your employees you will never be a good company manager.

Through inattention, effort is born and, with it, will and reason impose themselves as the strongest argument for change. But the transformation must come from surrender, never from effort or reason. Only delivery returns us to ourselves. And that is the most overlooked factor in the modern world.

There are too many methods, not so many to teach how to change, just to teach how to want to change. That is what Western schools teach. That change, transformation, must be born of effort. I repeat, I believe that transformation, attention and care must come from surrender, not so much from effort or reason. This is a proposal for a fracturing change to end fear, establishing the Caring Economy.

Foreword

How to change?

Many people are contacting me in the hope of seeing some of the most unfathomable mysteries of human life solved, a task that I consider to be far beyond my possibilities. Even so, whenever I can, I keep trying. They all revolve around the same issue: the human condition.

This is, in the chapter of economics, a theme that I consider structural and unavoidable. It is incomprehensible to think that we can have good decision-makers, good leaders, empty of humanity and self-knowledge. Or, even more incredible, having great business leaders who cannot, due to their exclusive and sole responsibility, even keep their own family together.

Faced with the essential questions, since the beginning of time, we are all prisoners of the same doubts, especially in a world where everything has become a mere formality, whose success depends on the correct completion of a standard form, on the trivialization of indignity and evil.

And that brought prostration and boredom to the decision-making environment, even in the most trivial matters. This explains so much suffering and fear in contemporary society. What is certain is that we have more to learn from nature than from civilization!

* * * * *

Paulo Vieira de Castro, MSc is a renowned Portuguese author in the field of awareness for organizations. He has authored and contributed to 7 books in this area: The Book of Pain and Suffering (2019); The Civilization of Fear (2017); Long live the crisis: the awakening of awareness in uncertain times (2014), Samurai Management - To Lead is to Serve (2013), Marketing In Change of Context (2012), Dharma Marketing: Spirituality in Business (2011), Economics and Spirituality : Reforming the Business World (2011).

The Tao of the Dow

His work has been published in some of the most prestigious journals in business such as HSM Management (Brazil), Época Negócios (Brazil), Marketeer (Portugal), Pronews (Brazil), ALSHOP NEWS (Brazil), Zen Energy (Portugal), Weekly Advertising and Marketing (Brazil). Castro developed the Doshu aspect of the Samurai Mental Training model. For over a decade, he has been active in teaching and collaborating in the areas of Strategic Management, Marketing and Communication with various graduate and post-graduate institutions.

Paulo has acted as a consultant in projects in various areas of business administration. Previously, Paulo served as Director of Organizational Well-Being at I-ACT, where he developed training and consulting for community, civic, educational and professional leaders based on the power of consciousness. Also, he have relevant political and social experience. He is a commissioner in the "Security Commission of the Porto City Council". Member of the National Political Commission of the "Party of People, Animals and Nature". Director of the event, "International Congress of Fear" (www.congressodomedo.pt).

*****

[1] The separation of subjects may take place at the level of State Secretaries.
[2] I propose the creation of a budget dedicated exclusively to well-being.

Editor's Preface

The Tao of the Dow demonstrates the crucial connection between consciousness and the economy. This compelling work reminds us that we can create a revolutionary shift in our personal finances, job satisfaction, and the greater economy, by simply moving our focus back to the things that really matter. As a society, we often make the mistake of viewing the economy as something that needs to be tamed or bowed to. However, when we fully understand that the economy is merely a tool to enhance creativity and facilitate community, the economy becomes a means of expanding well-being, rather than something we have to try to predict.

This collection of essays, articles, and interviews teaches us how to view economic laws through the right lens, and how to promote the leadership necessary to enable a new kind of marketplace. It encourages us to plumb the depths of our consciousness until the invisible forces that are the true economic determinants become apparent. The Tao of the Dow empowers us to take our rightful role in shaping our personal and professional lives to reflect greater freedom and personal satisfaction so that the workplace becomes an environment of innovation. We need to move out of the stultifying constraints of traditional economic principles and leadership so that the next generation will understand work to be a joyous outgrowth of human creativity and dignity. By equipping ourselves with mindfulness and consciousness-expanding techniques, we can live fulfilling and purposeful lives.

In order to have a successful economy, we need to reconnect with the kind of talent and fresh ideas that come organically from within, so that we're no longer struggling with the outer picture. Problem-solving skills can stem from a place beyond the rational mind, and from a place of ethical nobility. The call for a higher level of creativity is also the call for a more genuine interconnectedness between people. It may seem naive to discuss compassion and cooperation side by side

The Tao of the Dow

with economics in a seemingly competitive world; but sustainable growth is always achieved by those who are bold enough to value the people they lead and work with. Even the person at the bottom of the totem pole has opportunities to lead and facilitate change; and as we take advantage of these opportunities, however seemingly insignificant they may seem at the time, the unseen world around us responds with even greater opportunities.

In The Wealth of Nations, Adam Smith coined the well-known term 'The invisible hand' referring to the notion that an economy where people are free to pursue their needs will naturally result in an ideal marketplace where everyone benefits. There is an 'invisible hand' that regulates supply and demand. America has indeed reached unprecedented wealth as a nation by protecting economic freedom and letting this 'invisible hand' do the work of sustaining economic growth; but now imagine a society where people are even more conscious of what they really want as moral, creative, evolving beings. How much more so would this 'invisible hand' be able to guide us toward true prosperity both in our financial and personal lives? In fact, there is not only an 'invisible hand' but an unseen world, an extra-physical plane, that fuels our thoughts and even our bodies. Want to know what out-of-body experiences and energy techniques have to do with economics? Read on.

It's all too easy to get caught up in the daily grind of life and forget that we are here individually and collectively to make life-altering contributions. Let's not waste any more time succumbing to outmoded paradigms. Let this book be a light as we knock down societal constraints to become the free, wildly creative, empowered beings we were born to be.

~Consciousness Publishing

Author's Preface
Nelson Abreu, Los Angeles, April 20, 2020

The Tao of the Dow is the result of the slow articulation, as it emerged between 2012 and 2020, of my understanding of the two-way relationship between the world of the Mind and the everyday sphere of economic activity. At its core is a simple idea: the world's systems and assumptions that frame our decisions stem from the deep recesses of our Mind. If we change our Mind, we can change the Systems. Anything that exposes this relationship in practice becomes rather important in a world in crisis-opportunity.

I began organizing my ideas into a course in 2015 and the idea for the book came together in mid-2018. It really picked up in mid-2019. At no point did I expect to be writing this preface in the middle of a historic pandemic, looking at charts of record market gains next to spikes in COVID-19 deaths. "The economy" was doing well for a long time, while most people's quality of life seemed to be retreating.

The Gross Domestic Product had long shown that it could go up and up, alongside with the misery of populations. Our economies treat what is priceless (oxygen, love, kindness, honor, ethics, a nearly extinct species, one more year of life of a poor person) as worthless, because we cannot or do not measure it - we know something is wrong with this picture.

Now, with 27 million people (and counting) filing for unemployment in the US alone and most businesses forced to close, people are reflecting about the economy of tomorrow. This crisis has people thinking about the slower-moving train wreck of climate change, as well.

It is also apparent that a lot of economic activity does not involve the exchange of money at all: people are stepping up to donate their time and creations, using anything from sewing needles to 3D printing. Everyday people and, in particular, our honorable and brave first responders, are suffering even more from stress, fatigue, and anxiety.

The Tao of the Dow

At this very moment, Neuma Being is communicating with the local government to donate access to its Neuma Mind Spa well-being technology for use by first responders.

Meantime, the "other epidemic" of opioid addiction has revealed other ways in which the economy is ravaging communities -- and more ways in which mindfulness, lucid sleep and other heightened states can make a difference: pain management. Finally, innovators, civic and business leaders all over the world are reflecting about the future: there is a greater need for innovation and creativity: where do great ideas come from, if not the Mind?

I felt this was a book that wanted to be written and that almost had a mind of its own, but, frankly, I never guessed its ultimate timeliness. Like most people, I did not imagine our lives would grind to a stop like this. I am saddened by the suffering and death that is happening around the corner and around the world. I am also inspired by the best of the human spirit that is being exhibited and hopeful of what could emerge from this forced, collective spiritual retreat. We are learning to physically isolate ("social distance") and improve our hygiene, but also to distance socialize: using technology and our new-found "time" to have intimate moments of connection with friends and relatives.

This work includes wisdom from some of the people I've had the privilege of conversing with -- as well as my own insights from the realms of the Mind, Matter and in between. It follows my journey from mindful experience to emerging new economics and into technological applications. My wish is for you to find inspiration in these musings about our mental origins and glimpses of palpable, possible futures: inspiration to go within and find the well-being, creative insight, energy, clarity, courage and sense of Oneness: everything you need to go out there and make some "good trouble."

Notably, it does not include references to great conspiracies and dark forces from spiritual realms or outer space. There are no mentions of messianic, cataclysmic jumps in spiritual evolution from outside of us. If it is a foe you seek, look in the mirror and look around you. If it is a hero you seek, look in the mirror and look around you. This book is

Author's Preface

more a celebration of our individual and collective power to change. The evolution will not be televised or web streamed.

For nearly 15 years, from 1998 to 2012, I studied hypnosis, lucid dreams, out-of-body experiences, energy mindfulness, intuition, mindfulness and related phenomena -- along-side electrical engineering. I was initially drawn by scientific and philosophical curiosity about the mysteries of the mind and potential spiritual ramifications.

I stuck to the subject matter, because it profoundly affected my worldview (and that of those I educated) in powerful ways as a result of these experiences: reducing their fear of death; caring more about and feeling a greater connection to other living beings; seeking a more purpose-driven life and moving away from an overly materialistic paradigm.

Initially, my thinking was that I would help chart the way for the future of science and society through rather exotic work and by planting the seeds for change through workshops attended by a relatively small number of students: quality over quantity, depth over breadth. However, it became increasingly difficult to focus on spiritual, philosophical and scientific matters in a way that did not connect with the majority of people.

After years of experience and insight, I could see ramifications of the apparently "esoteric" work I had been steeped in and daily concerns of pollution and climate change; the 2008 market crash and rising inequality; and an accompanying erosion of civility and reason.

As a pragmatic individual with an engineer's mindset, I found myself increasingly drawn to emerging solutions: the circular economy; the doughnut economy; benefit corporations; the pluralist commonwealth; deliberative polling; direct democracy; digital currencies; agro-ecology; worker-owned cooperatives (I went as far as starting two such entities). The more I learned about "the economy" and the nature of money, the more I found myself peering back into the world of the Mind.

At the same time, I began an effort of developing a simpler way of discussing methods and insights related to the Mind. A new narrative,

The Tao of the Dow

language and approach was needed to show the everyday applications of Consciousness. I also began to show students and scholars of the Mind, how to make their work seem more pertinent to more people by connecting it to everyday worlds of home, the workplace, and government.

I co-founded companies that began bridging these two worlds to put my ideas to the test in the marketplace: do everyday people really value what I have to offer? Do I know how to translate this value? How can I (and others) have a larger-scale impact without listening and communicating effectively? This led me to the world of human-centered design for effective innovation with a Masters in innovation at University of Southern California.

Finally, this led me to where I started: engineering. Acting in part out of my genuine passion and on the advice of my late mentor Prof. Robert Jahn (former engineer dean at Princeton University), I began developing technologies that reveal everyday uses of consciousness-related knowledge.

I reduced talks, the research experimentation and articles and developed apps, hardware, and experiences that spoke to everyday people. Rather than talk about it, I set out to show it. If people experience benefits, they will be more persuaded than attending a lecture or reading a thesis -- if you can get people to do either in today's lower-attention-span world.

Today, my journey continues at Neumascape Studio and Neuma Being, as a confluence of design, business, technology and Mind. I am determined to normalize and generalize the sub-conscious, mindfulness, lucid sleep, and other heightened states as means of furthering well-being, creative insight and, when you are fortunate, life-changing cognitive shifts.

The crisis that transpires as I type these words has sharpened my own understanding. It has never been clearer to me that the demand for consciousness-based solutions is high. Also, it's never been more important for those who trek through the worlds of consciousness and spirituality to learn a thing or two from the worlds of business, design and technology. I sincerely hope you find this collection of musings

Author's Preface

thought-provoking. It just might change the way you think about money, the economy, work, technology and their relationship to our Being or the Self.

The Tao of the Dow

Table of Contents

1. The Tao of the Dow & the Mind of Money 25
2. From Plato's Cave to Global Change 37
3. Awe: Transpersonal Experience 43
4. Conscious Leadership 51
5. Zero Cost Economics 57
6. Smart Cities, Healthy Cities: City as a Health Ecosystem 65
7. Vitalism: Beyond Capitalism & Communism 69
8. What Steve Jobs Understood About Consciousness and Design 73
9. Internal Reality: Emerging Conscious Tech 79
10. Innovations in Consciousness Research 101
11. Neuma Being: Well-Being Technology 127
12. Where Do Great Ideas Come From? 149
13. Consciousness Hacking the Nervous System 155
14. The Promise and Peril of Tech 159
15. The Commons in the World to Come 169
16. Manifesto 175

The Tao of the Dow

1. The Tao of the Dow & the Mind of Money

The Tao of the Dow Part 1: Consciousness & Economics

To some, consciousness may seem like an abstract subject of study, devoid of practical consequence for what most people value in their day-to-day lives. For instance, what does the possibility suggested by near-death experiences that reality could extend beyond the material realm have to do with the Gross Domestic Product?

Financial news discusses GDP, interest rates, the value of stocks, the price of oil, and other numerical parameters. However, underneath all these apparently objective matters, we find flows of information in a power struggle between various agents and interest groups. Here, rule intentions, strategies, actions, reactions, words, interpretations, prognostications, models of reality...These are, in turn, based on attitudes and patterns of behavior, which are ultimately rooted in what we value or prioritize in accordance to our individual natures and how we respond or affect the overall culture (collective unconscious, zeitgeist, morphic field, information field, noosphere, or holothosene).

If individual consciousness changes as a result of transformative experiences like out-of-body or near-death experiences, their paradigm-shift may reflect on what they value: rather than material things and a will to power over others, they may shift toward enriching experiences and a will to power over their own immaturities and weaknesses - the darker and ignorant aspects of their own nature - and to develop their internal powers, knowledge, capacities or qualities. Such transformative experiences can lead one to foster cooperation and increased well-being and goodwill for others as oneself.

A post-materialist, non-reductionist, collaborative paradigm centered on human potential associated with such transpersonal experiences would certainly result in a very different economic system from past failed models and current models in crisis.

We do not have to look to psi phenomena for transformative experience. When humankind took the first picture of Earth from outer space, it revealed to itself the beauty of its Home, its Space Ship, and the ignorance of divisiveness and ecocide. As consumers, people in developed nations are less apathetic to child and slave labor and anti-ecological practices, holding companies accountable to a higher ethical standard. The sharing, connectivity and neutrality of the Internet, once tasted, is now worth fighting for and people are not willing to relinquish it to particular interests. Instead, they are disrupting old ways of being and doing, through sharing ideas, resources and creations.

As the collective conscience evolves, so does the economy - often as a result planted by a few pioneers of conscience and vision, the result of our own intellectual and spiritual evolution and by crises and other events that mark us, accelerated by connectivity technology. Economics are rooted in human behavior - the most influential thinkers on economics from Adam Smith to Karl Marx understood this.

As technology takes over more and more jobs that were once performed by humans, attributes like creativity and innovation (traits associated with lucid dreamers and conscious projectors, for example) become more valuable. On the other hand, the means of production and its associated wealth are becoming more and more concentrated on a smaller population. More and more people are

The Tao of the Dow & the Mind of Money

becoming redundant to economic production. Technological breakthroughs and social benefits that can extend the quality and duration of life are often quite expensive. This is forcing societies to evaluate, not the price of gold (which is partially objectively and partially subjectively determined), but the value of a human life. Is the worth of a human being determined by his or her accumulation, expenditure, or production of wealth?

What is truly important in life? Will you defend only your own short-term security? Attempt to secure your membership in corporate, local or national elites that defend their own power and freedoms?
With smaller tax bases, people are less able to rely on nation-states and are looking increasingly to contribute to their community for human security, because it is the right thing to do and because our connectivity ensures that someone else's problem becomes your problem sooner or later, even in other countries. How can we foster individual liberty and potential, while caring for the liberty and potential of others?

The highest human principles value dignity, virtue, liberty, knowledge, relationships, human potential, and well-being. Our actions show that our values are not always in line with our principles. Why not? This is the realm of consciousness science and allied academic fields like psychology, sociology, anthropology, history, philosophy, neuroscience, and political science. Specialists from these and other fields converged in Portugal for the International Congress on Consciousness. The experiences, experiments and theories discussed at the ICC are all centered on the nature of consciousness and our conception of reality: the root-level of all our manifestations, which affect our ethics or values, and patterns of behavior and attitudes. In turn, these provide the ubiquitous, nearly-invisible, but powerful framework that underlies what, how and why we do what we do individually, socially and as a global village.

As "Samurai Management" and "Dharma Marketing" author and ICC panel moderator Paulo Vieira de Castro says "we are born empty-handed and we die empty-handed," so the accumulation of capital and material goods is clearly a pathology. Castro also reminds us that

The Tao of the Dow

a cow in a pasture appears content, because it is expected to act as a cow - no more, no less. Capital went from a means to an end, but human unhappiness prevails, because humans are in dissonance with their own nature as an interconnected consciousness in a progress of self-realization. Sharing, collaboration, applied self-knowledge and growing with others, must replace hording, separation, competition and self-ignorance. Change your consciousness, change your world.

With the greater part of rich people, the chief enjoyment of riches consists in the parade of riches.
ADAM SMITH

Natural science will in time incorporate into itself the science of man, just as the science of man will incorporate into itself natural science: there will be one science.
KARL MARX

Watch your thoughts, they become words;
watch your words, they become actions;
watch your actions, they become habits;
watch your habits, they become character;
watch your character, for it becomes your destiny.
FRANK OUTLAW

Your beliefs become your thoughts,
Your thoughts become your words,
Your words become your actions,
Your actions become your habits,
Your habits become your values,
Your values become your destiny.
MAHATMA GANDHI

The Tao of the Dow & the Mind of Money

Happiness is when what you think, what you say, and what you do are in harmony.
MAHATMA GANDHI

The process by which money is created is so simple that the mind is repelled. Where something so important is involved, a deeper mystery seems only decent.
JOHN KENNETH GALBRAITH (economist and advisor to John F Kennedy in his 1971 book Money)

Don't think money does everything or you are going to end up doing everything for money.
VOLTAIRE

The power of markets is enormous, but they have no inherent moral character. We have to decide how to manage them... For all these reasons, it is plain that markets must be tamed and tempered to make sure they work to the benefit of most citizens. And that has to be done repeatedly, to ensure that they continue to do so.
JOSEPH E. STIGLITZ, The Price of Inequality

The only true and sustainable prosperity is shared prosperity.
JOSEPH E. STIGLITZ

The Tao of the Dow Part 2: Spirituality & Economics - Rudolph Steiner on Interdependence

Rudolf Steiner (1861-1925) was an Austrian philosopher and scientist whose work influenced a number of fields, including agriculture, education, medicine, science, architecture, spiritual development, and social theory. Biodynamic farming and Waldorf schools are contemporary examples inspired by Steiner. In 1922, he gave a course of lectures on economics.

The Tao of the Dow

While not constituting an endorsement of his entire philosophy, we share some summaries of his work in economics for general culture, as we explore the link between money and consciousness.

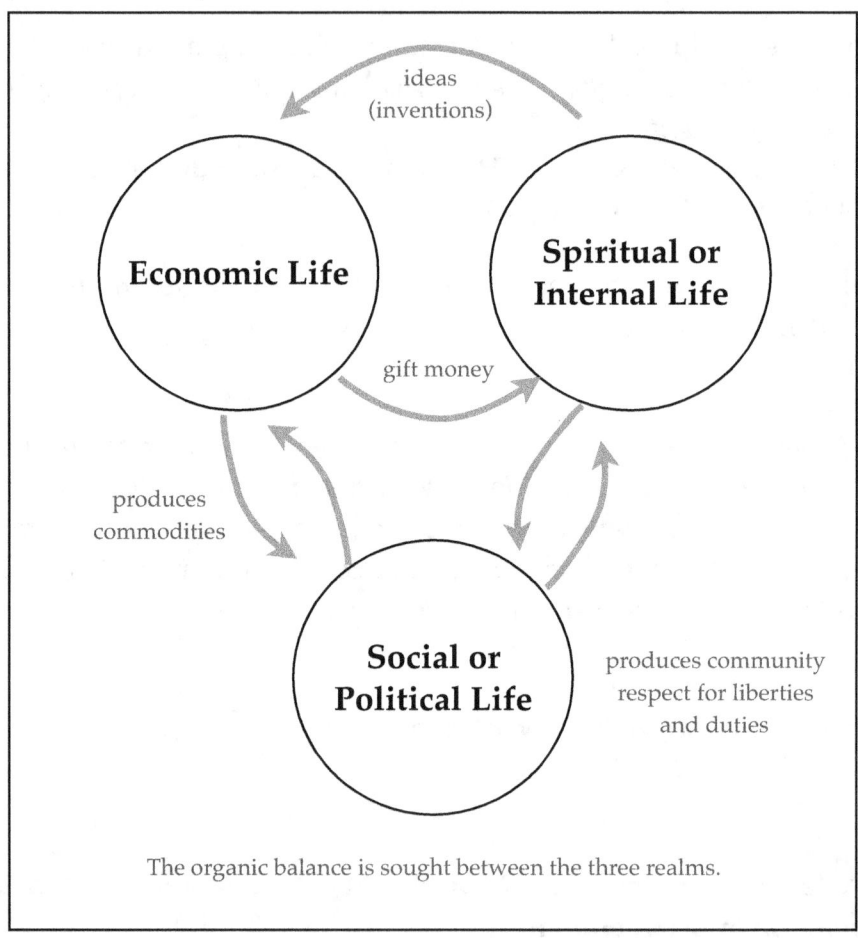

The organic balance is sought between the three realms.

Social threefolding is an ideology from Rudolf Steiner suggesting the progressive independence of society's economic, political and cultural institutions. It aims to foster:
- human rights and equality in political life,
- freedom in cultural life (art, science, religion, education, the media),
- associative cooperation in economic life.

The Tao of the Dow & the Mind of Money

Steiner held it to be socially destructive when one of the three spheres attempts to dominate the others; For example, theocracy means a cultural impulse dominates; unregulated and socially irresponsible varieties of capitalism allow economic interests to dominate; and totalitarianism means political agendas dominate culture and economic life.

Rudolph Steiner on Economics and Spirituality:
http://www.rudolfsteinerweb.com/
http://www.threefolding.org/
http://www.tripartizione.it/articoli/
GGPreparata_Perishable_Money_in_a_Threefold_Commonwealth.pdf

If you understand Spanish, you may find these lectures of interest as well, featuring Joan Melé of Triodos Bank:
http://youtube.com/watch?v=6txm08NAkQg
http://youtube.com/watch?v=UK3hC1xxHQM

To Steiner, interdependence is at the root of most spiritual traditions, and increasingly serves as the foundation of scientific inquiry, including systems theory and quantum mechanics. In the sphere of economics, Rudolf Steiner described it as "associative." He understood money to be a bridge – a circulatory system – invented to connect human beings in relationships of service.

Steiner proposed that societies are structured through spiritual life, with educational and cultural aspects, the legal life, with political and social aspects, and economic life, with production, consumption and distribution. These three founding members of the society obey their own laws and ideals: individual freedom in cultural and spiritual life; legal equality in life and in the state; and fraternity or solidarity in economic life.

Steiner encouraged us to strive for a less hierarchical, more networked approach to business leadership. Like all philosophers, Steiner was all too human and a product of his time. For instance, a BBC piece has raised questions about how much of his outdated ideas such as those regarding race make their way into schools inspired on his work. It could be argued that Steiner still has much to offer to our contemporary world, but as with any approach or body of knowledge, one must use discernment, a critical mind and apply - put to the test - only what may be constructive.

The Tao of the Dow Part 3: "We need a powerful new story"

Richard Schiffman is the author of two biographies as well as a journalist whose work has appeared in The New York Times, Salon, The Washington Post, The Christian Science Monitor, The Huffington Post, and on NPR and Monitor Radio. In this article published in Yes! Magazine and re-published by Truthout, Schiffman defends that "we need a powerful new story that we are a part of nature and not separate from it."

The article mentions a wonderful documentary project called The Overview Effect, which features several astronauts attempting to describe their awe-inspiring, paradigm-shifting, exoplanetary experiences. Among them is the 6th man to land on the moon and IONS co-founder Dr. Edgar Mitchell who describes a heightened state of awareness and interconnectedness triggered by the sight of the Earth from outerspace. As orbital tourism nears commercial feasibility, we can look forward to more and more people seeing the Earth as it is: a glistening blue, living space ship with a thin, thin protective layer that we must protect, without borders, but with more and more visible scars. It is no wonder that, as Neil deGrasse Tyson posits, the ecological movement (and interest in science and engineering) got a huge boost after the first images of Earth from outer space entered our collective holothosene, zeitgeist, morphic field, or collective information field.

The paradigm shift afforded by lucid projections of the consciousness or out-of-body experiences is just as impactful. It is similar in the way that we see our "home" from the outside and have the chance to reconsider it. It also broadens our sense of universalism and triggers serious questioning of reality and our place in it. Both experiences bridge theory and visceral experience, as beautifully described in the film The Overview Effect. In other words, unlike the outdated view of the OBE as a dissociative experience, it is quite the opposite. Both the "out of body" and "out of planet" experiences are profoundly integrative, expanding our sense of oneness with fellow beings, with the very fabric of multidimensional Reality.

The difference is that we tend to identify too much with this body and not enough with our life-sustaining planet. The projection shows us that while the fragile, mortal, breathing, walking, sleeping, hungry, hormonal, instinctual body is a precious vessel for us to evolve in this dimension, it is certainly not who or what we are. In fact, we realize that we are much more vast and eternal than this useful scaffold meat suit: at least as cosmic as the physical cosmos that surrounds our Earth.

Other voices are promoting a new story for humanity like Charles Eisenstein, a teacher, speaker, and writer focusing on themes of civilization, consciousness, money, and human cultural evolution. They envision a new economy based on insights from consciousness development.

The International Academy of Consciousness is also a part of this movement. In 1992, IAC president Wagner Alegretti delivered a speech at the United Nations' Earth Summit to elucidate the link between consciousness and ecology. As we witness the continual detriment of our "space-ship" Earth, we can ask why there is still insufficient will to reverse the trend. Underpinning our behavior is a worldview or paradigm, a story that we have internalized. The predominant paradigm can be characterized as materialistic, mechanistic, or reductionist.

In other words, we tend to understand humans, animals, trees, rivers, air, water, and the rest of the Earth as material things, or resources for material motivations. Even though we may have certain principles that state otherwise (from religion, from modern science like the 100-year-old quantum physics, our internal compass or philosophy, our senses), when we are limited to physical senses, this limited view of the world seems to convey that all is matter; that life is short; that we are on our own and must follow our own immediatist best interest in a competitive world.

There is perhaps no better demonstration of the folly of human conceits than this distant image of our tiny world. To me, it underscores our responsibility to deal more kindly with one another, and to preserve and cherish the pale blue dot, the only home we've ever known.
CARL SAGAN

Experiences like seeing the Earth from outer space, clairvoyance or projection of the consciousness (out-of-body experience), however, literally give us a new perspective, a new consciousness-centric or consciential paradigm. In other words, it demonstrates that Life is not a thing. We are not the body, ecological systems are not mere resources, the experience of enjoying the sight of a beautiful mountain is not worthless, even if it is not tangible or monetized.

With this new cosmology, we understand ourselves in a more integrated way, as part of a cosmic ecosystem, a cosmic family. We understand that actions (even our thoughts and intentions) have inexorable consequences and we think in a more long-term fashion. We understand that we are eternal and that we have more than just this life: not only should we preserve the Earth for future generations, we may be part of those future generations.

As we disconnect from the consensus trance, from the rat race, we naturally seek more authentic and lucid sources of purpose, of meaning. Rather than being driven by fear, we discover new motivations: the continual drive to improve ourselves, to learn and to advance the well-being and evolution of our fellow Beings.

Earth provides enough to satisfy every man's needs, but not every man's greed.
MOHANDAS GANDHI

The Tao of the Dow & the Mind of Money

The greatest illusion of this world is the illusion of separation. Once what the story our world is built on reflects the reality of interconnection, we will be on a true path towards sustainability.
CHARLES EISENSTEIN

The Tao of the Dow Part 4: Ethical Consumers

We see signs that people are starting to realize the potential of conscious economic collaboration with the sharing economy, democratic or cooperative companies, and the world of collaborative social apps.

Consumer behavior and investment preferences have begun to shift – and that shift is accelerating. We see pressure on companies for fair trade, safe and child-free labor, and greener practices. Where companies fail to do this, social media is proving a formidable force for awareness: the beginning of change.

Case in point: international tobacco industry and the #jeffwecan campaign (warning: offensive language and even more offensive business practices portrayed); the recent net neutrality ruling in the US, pressured by petitions that crashed the servers of the FCC; and the growing, global campaign to #divest from companies related to polluting energy companies.

A recent editorial on EnergyBiz argues that staying in tune with the changing moral compass can be a matter of survival for companies, which need to maintain the trust and respect of their customers - something the energy industry has not had a stellar record doing in the last decades.

As more aware consumers see the ramifications of where and how they spend their money, the energy and other industries are facing a new generation which has ethical expectations of the companies from which they purchase products and services.

This awareness is spreading to where they work, where they live and where they save or invest money. Students are leading the charge

The Tao of the Dow

by pressuring the funds of their universities to invest in a way that is more coherent with scientific and ethical principles.

Dissatisfaction with the financial sector and its corrupting influence on politics has been rampant since the global crises erupted in 2008 with large protests in several countries, but few seem willing or able to articulate the spiritual or consciential roots of the crises. One notable exception was a former finance minister and professor of economics who posited that consciousness was the root level of the economy, and that, hence, mid- and long-term improvements must start there.

What other signs of rising ethical standards and its influence in economics have you seen?

Resource: Would you give up Google for $17,000 a year?
The Federal Reserve wants to know:
https://apple.news/AAmzg4SXnSZ6xK3DS6kQIUg

2. From Plato's Cave to Global Change

Our senses give us a false sense of solidity of matter and hide the fact that it is only the tip of the iceberg of a spectrum of consciousness realities revealed through transpersonal experiences.

By changing our worldview, we become agents of positive, structural change, helping co-create the better future we know is possible, rather than being victimized by undesirable change.

For the majority of human history, we have considered the human spirit, soul, self, or mind a self-evident and fundamental part of reality. The material realm was often regarded as less of a reality than consciousness, or at best an extension or reflection of it. With the progress of empirical science, however, a conflict developed between those who dared question orthodox doctrines and the religious power that defended such dogma. A relative truce was achieved by establishing mutually exclusive magisteria: the material realm could be investigated by the scientific spirit and matters of the spirit were to be left to the clergy.

Religious authority's censorship and abuse of power led scientists away from studying the nature of our internal reality, limiting to phenomena that can be physically posited, until subjective reality was all but rejected in a new kind of bias and censorship. Consciousness was increasingly considered an illusion, an imaginary ghost in the biological billiard ball machine, a relatively unimportant secondary phenomenon of the brain.

It is worth pointing out that many of the pioneers of physics like Newton, Einstein and Bohm did not limit their world view to the observable physical world and were curious about the subjective realm. While great technological progress has been achieved through Newtonian-Cartesian materialistic science, its usefulness has declined with the rise of quantum physics a century ago.

After a reductionist detour of about two centuries, the idea that consciousness is real, fundamental, and irreducible is resurgent. However, this time, consciousness is returning to the centre as a result of the application of the scientific spirit, including parapsychology and contemporary consciousness science, rather than religious thought.

The current planetary crisis is further demonstrative of the inadequacy of the materialistic worldview as a paradigm upon which to build civilizations. Not only is the ailing materialistic paradigm challenged by the physics and consciousness research of the last century, materialism lacks internal, logical consistency. For all the claims of scientism that the human essence does not exist, that we are just pieces of matter, it reaches such conclusions through experience and thought, which take place in the realm of consciousness. Truly, only consciousness could be simultaneously this clever and unwise as to negate itself!

Why is this pathological, destructive paradigm so persistent? Our senses give us a false sense of solidity of matter and hide the fact that it is only the tip of the iceberg of a spectrum of consciousness realities revealed through transpersonal experiences. In other words, we do not react to things we know in theory the same way as things that we experience viscerally. We are moved by experiences, not data or facts. We are moved by the image of a single, beached refugee child, and not by statistics that we cannot comprehend. Consciousness science – but above all, consciousness practices –allow us to become more perceptive and achieve new levels of awareness, ethics and maturity.

Plato's allegory of the cave:

A group of prisoners, who have lived chained to the wall of a cave all of their lives, face a blank wall, watching shadows projected on the wall from things passing in front of a fire behind them. The shadows are as close as the prisoners get to viewing reality. Plato explains how the philosopher is like a prisoner who is freed from the cave and comes to understand that the shadows on the wall do not make up reality at all, for he can perceive the true form of reality rather than the mere shadows seen by the prisoners.

Transformative experiences like near-death and out-of-body experiences allow us to look beyond the shadows of Plato's allegory of the cave. Experiencers tend to reduce their fear of death, to achieve a greater level of altruism, universalism, intuition, problem solving, tranquility, introspection and sense of purpose. The cognitive shifts they afford help us realize we view reality through limiting and distorting filters. By doing so, we can see ourselves and our lives from a multi-dimensional and integrative perspective. By changing our worldview, we become agents of positive change, helping to co-create the better future we know is possible, rather than being victimized by undesirable change. Even when we are faced with troubling personal or social situations, the same integrative, multi-dimensional perspective based on personal experiences of insight beyond the material realm can give us strength. We can remain relatively positive and lucid so as not to succumb to and spread fear, hatred, self-loathing or manipulation, remaining a voice for serenity.

At the deepest levels, all human activity is rooted on our values, attitudes and patterns of behavior, which are in turn based on our state of consciousness. As such, our reality may be seen as an extension of the consciousness. Consciousness may be described as an organizing intelligent principle that is in a continuous process of individual and inter-connected, collective evolution, over a number of existences with and without a body. Relationships and interactions with others provide the context and means for the evolution of consciousness. As more people from different disciplines and aspects of civilization experience reality beyond the materialistic confines, from art and architecture to ethics and policy-making, our collective system begins to shift. Many of the world's problems come from the perspective we are on our own in a competitive world and that nature, life and people are things to be exploited. When we see ourselves as consciousness that stems from beyond the physical body, this continuity and connection between ourselves, our bodies, spirits and all living things becomes apparent.

With this knowledge, life, the environment, and most other things in life become more valuable and precious. Through extraordinary human experiences and related scientific evidence, we can see ourselves as a multi-dimensional consciousness in the process of evolution along with other beings. With this realization, we become more connected in a cosmic way to our fellow human beings and the priority becomes the well-being and development of individuals, communities, and the human family as a whole: human knowledge, abilities, intelligences, ethics, maturity, character, cooperation, and integral health. Well-being and development through cooperation take center stage, rather than competitive accumulation or growth of material wealth. A major pseudo-scientific fallacy of contemporary systems is revealed: we seek to manage civilization on the basis of measurements like GDP and interest rates, while what matters most – things such as love, happiness, personal growth, serenity, awe – simply cannot be measured in dollars and similar units.

Until recently the future used to be an optimistic concept, but most people now live with anxiety regarding the future. We live in a world with accelerating technological change and its associated increasing unemployment, uncertain geopolitical scenarios, periodic financial crises, and more frequent and powerful ecological disasters. It is not that we necessarily lack technical solutions, but rather feel jaded about the generalized ineffectiveness of our so-called leaders to address our critical and most fundamental needs.

There is a growing awareness that the challenges we face as citizens and as a species are not going to be solved by a given personality or political party. We face structural problems that cannot only be addressed by system change, but that comes from deep paradigm change. Lincoln is often credited with the saying that "the best way to predict the future is to to create it," and the Nobel laureate Dennis Gabor has said that "the future cannot be predicted, but futures can be invented." Indeed, we cannot look to the elites that perversely benefit from our sinking ship, but must rather find our leaders in the mirror.

As more individuals proactively change their own worldview and make healthy changes in their core, the more they promote change through their actions and collaborations, the more they 'hack' the prevailing morphic field (the sphere of human thought, information field, zeitgeist, collective unconscious)–and the closer we get to a tipping point for regional and global change.

The Tao of the Dow

3. Awe: Transpersonal Experience
as Catalyst to Post-Reductionism and Toward Consciousness or Life-Centered Civilization

Part I:

For the majority of human history, we have considered the human spirit, soul, self, or mind a self-evident and fundamental part of Reality. The material realm was often regarded as less of a reality than consciousness, or at best an extension or reflection of it. With the progress of empirical science, however, a conflict developed between those who dared question orthodox doctrines and the religious power that defended such dogma. A relative truce was achieved by establishing mutually-exclusive magisteria: the material realm could be investigated by the scientific spirit and matters of the spirit were to be left to the clergy.

Religious authority's censorship and abuse of power led scientists away from studying the nature of our internal reality, limiting science to phenomena that can be physically posited, until subjective reality was all but rejected in a new kind of bias and censorship: an epistemological fundamentalism often referred to as scientism. Consciousness was increasingly considered an illusion, an imaginary ghost in the biological billiard ball machine, an epiphenomenon of the brain.

It is worth pointing out that many of the pioneers of quantum physics (as well as the likes of Newton, Descartes, Einstein) did not limit their world view to the observable physical world and were curious about the subjective realm. While great technological progress has been achieved through Newtonian-Cartesian material science, it's usefulness has deteriorated with the rise of quantum physics a century ago.

After a reductionist detour of about two centuries, the idea that consciousness is real, fundamental, and irreducible is resurgent. However, this time consciousness is returning to the center as a result of the application of the scientific spirit, including parapsychology and contemporary consciousness science, rather than religious thought. The current planetary crisis is further demonstrative of the inadequacy of the materialistic worldview as a paradigm upon which to build civilizations. Not only is the ailing materialistic paradigm challenged by the physics and consciousness research of the last century, materialism lacks internal, logical consistency as elucidated by idealism philosophers like Bernardo Kastrup.

We can also look to remarks by speculative realism philosophers like Graham Harman on the folly of reductionist scientism:

"[T]here's a more insidious form of human-centric ontology, as found in many versions of scientism. On the one hand, scientism insists that human consciousness is nothing special, and should be naturalized just like everything else. On the other hand, it also wants to preserve knowledge as a special kind of relation to the world quite different from the relations that raindrops and lizards have to the world. Another of putting it… for all their gloating over the fact that people are pieces of matter just like everything else, they also want to claim that the very status of that utterance is somehow special. For them, raindrops know nothing and lizards know very little, and some humans are more knowledgeable than others. This is only possible because thought is given a unique ability to negate and transcend immediate experience, which inanimate matter is never allowed to do in such theories, of course. In short, for all its noir claims that the human doesn't exist, it elevates the structure of human thought to the ontological pinnacle."

The curriculum of educational activities and the research programs at International Academy of Consciousness are based on a paradigm that recognizes consciousness as more than an ephemeral result of biological evolution, which is itself widely considered to be an accidental outcome of matter-energy. The Consciential Paradigm gives central stage to consciousness - after all, all we observe and experience is through and in consciousness. It does not dismiss the material reality and the biological systems. Rather, it contextualizes it in a more holistic, integrative, multi-level "outer" cosmos that extends from physical reality into other subtle aspects of reality experienced through chi, near-death experiences, out-of-body experiences, cosmic consciousness and more. The "outer" appears more and more like an extension of the "inner," each giving meaning to the other. Without the observing, participating consciousness, "outer" reality loses any meaning as reality outside of observation and is not something we can ascertain. Without the "inner" reality, our microcosm and our shared experiences, a reductionist, mechanistic account of reality is clearly limited.

Though stubbornly holding on, reductionist materialism has been in decline for over a century. However, why is the pathological, destructive mono-materialist paradigm so persistent? Our senses give us a false sense of solidity of matter and hide the fact that it is only the tip of the iceberg of a spectrum of consciousness realities. However, as a result of transpersonal experiences, we become more perceptive and able to transcend the usual limits of human awareness, ethics and maturity.

We can step out of our physical and solid world and look out through another lens. By doing so, we can see ourselves and our lives from a different perspective and when we come back, our worldview is shifted and changed. As worldviews change, so do all disciplines and aspects of civilization, from art and architecture to ethics and economics. The ramifications touch and inform all of our problems on earth. Many of the world's problems come from the human-centered perspective that nature and life are things; they are to be used and then thrown away. When we see ourselves as consciousness that exists outside the physical body, this continuity and connection between ourselves, our bodies, spirits, and all living things becomes apparent.

With this knowledge, life, the environment, and most other things in life, become more valuable and precious. Through extraordinary human experiences and related scientific evidence, we can see ourselves as a multi-dimensional consciousness in the process of evolution along with other beings. With this realization, we become more connected in a cosmic way to our fellow human beings and the priority becomes the well-being and development of individuals, communities, and the human family as a whole: human knowledge, abilities, intelligences, ethics, maturity, character, cooperation, and integral health.

Part II:

The Overview Effect is a related phenomenon that features a similar paradigm shift. Several astronauts describe their awe-inspiring, transformative exoplanetary experiences. As orbital tourism nears commercial feasibility, we can look forward to more and more people seeing the Earth as it is: a glistening blue, living space ship with a thin protective layer, without borders, but with more and more visible scars. It is no wonder that, as science educator Neil deGrasse Tyson often posits, the ecological and humanitarian movements (and interest in science and engineering) got a huge boost after the first images of Earth from outer space entered the global consciousness, collective unconscious, planetary holothosene, zeitgeist, morphic field, or information field.

The impact afforded by lucid projections of the consciousness or out-of-body experiences is at least as impactful. It is similar in the way that we see our "home" from the outside and have the chance to reconsider it. It also broadens our sense of universalism and triggers serious questioning of reality and our place in it. Both experiences bridge theory and visceral experience, as beautifully described in the aforementioned film. In other words, unlike the outdated view of the OBE as a dissociative or even narcissistic experience, it is quite the opposite. Both the "out of body" and "out of planet" experiences are profoundly integrative, expanding our sense of oneness with fellow beings, with the very fabric of multidimensional Reality.

The difference is that we tend to identify too much with this individual body and not enough with our life-sustaining planet. The projection shows us that while the fragile, mortal, breathing, walking, sleeping, hungry, hormonal, instinctual body is a precious vessel for us to evolve in this realm, it is certainly not the totality of who or what we are. In fact, we realize that we are much more vast and eternal than this useful scaffolding-meat suit: we are at least as cosmic as the physical cosmos that surrounds our Earth.

The emerging life-affirming, consciousness-centric paradigm sees consciousness as central to Reality. Consciousness, here, is used in its broadest sense, as a technical synonym for our essence, intelligence principle, Self, soul, or the bios in biology – the driving force of living beings itself; that which we are beyond the manifestations or vehicles of the consciousness like genetics, the brain, the body as a whole, or even the so-called chi, astral and mental/causal bodies that have been discussed for thousands of years: pre-historic shamans of animistic cultures, Vedic philosophers of ancient India, Judean mystics, Egyptian clerics, early Buddhist monks, all the way to contemporary leading-edge scientists starting in the 18th century with the likes of Emmanuel Swedenborg.

Based on more than speculation, this multidimensional and multiexistential view arises from actual experiences like the projection of the consciousness (astral projection), near-death experience, past life recall, clairvoyance, telepathy and mediumship which reveal that the consciousness is not limited to the material reality and that we oscillate between "physical" and "extraphysical" states: lives in a body (intraphysical period) and without one (extraphysical period or intermissive period).

Part III:

When confronted with these facts and "para-facts" from their own experiences, individuals often develop a significantly different "story" or worldview than the one that prevails in societies throughout the world. Even though many believe in an afterlife, their behavior does not reflect that. Once we understand that birth and death are transitions akin to awakening and sleeping, part of a continual development, each presenting important opportunities for growth and assistance of fellow beings who are not as separate or different as they may seem, we are led more and more to a life of continual positive self-improvement, including ethics, inner balance and self-mastery; a life of increasing selflessness and wide-reaching service, with a "long view" of all aspects of life. Death, then, does not provoke fear, anymore than sleep. We need not seek immortality: we are already immortal. However, our biological corpus and the current circumstances remain ephemeral and can be seized for furthering maturity and well-being of self and others: ever more complex, ordered and in tune with the laws of the cosmos. We discover there is no heaven or hell, only choices to make and repercussions to learn from in consciential evolution.

Fear is easy to manipulate and people that are afraid can be targets for malicious manipulation and influence. Free of this mother-of-all-fears, we are able to make better and more rational decisions. Attempting and having access to out-of-body experiences and other psi abilities can set us on a journey of trying to understand this life. We have this glimpse into something considered unusual, a different world that most people are not aware of, we will come back with questions and a new perspective on life. We will be more curious and the insights obtained can enrich all areas of human activity.

In other dimensions, just like in ours, thoughts and intentions have consequence, they attract things and people. This is sometimes called the law of attraction, and in the astral dimensions we are able to see this much easier and in a more immediate fashion. Soon, we realize how vital it is to promote the quality of and monitor changes in our thoughts, intentions, ethics, emotions, mood, the state of our body and chi. As we become more aware of our influence on others and ethical principles, we become more virtuous. We can become less less vulnerable to undue external influence, as well, advancing toward a total, permanent imperturbability (intrusionlessness).

So, while not feared, death remains a sort of looming deadline, providing some positive incentive to examine the current opportunities this type of existence provides. It also invites us to think about what kind of intermissive period (between physical lives) and next physical life we might like to have and what we can do in this life before we reach that "finish line," perhaps with tremendous satisfaction for the inner growth, relationship, intellectual and altruistic achievements and challenges overcome, for the artifacts or systems of knowledge and assistance left behind, and the depth and number of lives touched in and out-of-body.

Such a worldview may take a long time to become widespread. However, more daring and lucid individuals can develop a more multidimensional self-awareness, which can turn them into the life-affirming, visionary, ethical, universalistic, courageous leaders we need today to overcome the crises underpinned by the outdated paradigms. Awakening to psi abilities is only the beginning. How might you apply your multi-level awareness? Which issues could you tackle? Which area of knowledge will you advance? Have you planned something before you were even born? Your existential program can be as unique as you are. Here's to getting started, discovering it or taking it to the next level. Enjoy the challenge of Multidimensional Life and its gift of choice, of love, of beauty, of surprise, of challenge, of strangeness, of awe.

The Tow of the Dow

4. Conscious Leadership

By Mohammadreza Bashiri, BSEE, MBA, PE, Ed.D.

The concept of Conscious Leadership within the Organizational Well-Being framework pays close attention to genuine care and rapport and the quality of the organizational environment. It's important that team members feel safe: because you care about them and also to bring out the best in them.

Woodrow Wilson was not without his flaws, but his words on the purpose of life have left an indelible mark in my life. He posits that we are not alive "merely to make a living," but rather "to enable the world to live more amply, with greater vision, with a finer spirit of hope and achievement." He believed we are here "to enrich the world" and that we impoverish ourselves if we omit. His words inspired me to continuously seek to expand my awareness and sense of purpose and service.

My academic and professional experience in engineering, education, leadership and human resources has led me to understand that I can do my small but non-transferable duty to mankind by playing a role in developing leaders who can inspire and enable others to enrich the world. Our planet is facing global challenges partly due to a failure of leadership.

The world has immense resources, talented and inspired individuals, emerging technical and organizational solutions, but our leaders have been largely unable to translate all the potential of a highly connected world to address our fundamental needs.

More than ever, our world needs competent leaders in all sectors and levels of society, especially in our age of communications and as cities and organizations grow in importance compared to the traditional, centralized power of nation-states. What kind of leaders can bring out the best in the interconnected world of individuals, communities, and organizations towards greater well-being?
I am driven to be part of the solution and to inspire others to do the same, enhancing global well-being, rooted in caring for each other, by promoting health, a sense of purpose, autonomy, mastery, and authentic relationships in a caring environment.

To bring out the best and the most in people, my leadership philosophy prioritizes Organizational Well-Being. This requires a primary focus not on the outcome, but on the first principles, obtaining the desired outcomes as a result. Rather than focus primarily on Key Performance Indicators or even behaviors, Conscious Leadership seeks to understand how everything stems from one's mind or consciousness. If you are able to affect this deep level and to connect with people at this level, through genuine caring, it is possible to affect their consciousness: the source level of their attitudes, ethics, values and patterns of behavior.

That is why for me, love is everything. Love is the basis of my philosophy and purpose of life. No matter what you do, where you are, how you perform and whom you work with, starting from a place of love is essential.

Leading the people by their heart has meant fostering friendship in the organization, considering co-workers as family members, treating clients as human beings, being accountable to environment, making people feel safe, and developing your people. This will only be possible when the leader is full of a love for all things that is reflected in the organization.

As a leader, I have tried to help my people love their job and find a meaningful purpose in what they do and foster the notion of love in the organizations which I have lead.

My leadership philosophy is based on Well-being. Well-being, put simply, is what most people desire: physical and mental health and happiness. I believe that organizations that sincerely promote and care about team member wellness and happiness perform better in the long run, because members feel safe, cared for and motivated.

Leaders can promote well-being throughout their organization by developing rapport, healthy habits, a safe or caring environment, a sense of purpose, sufficient autonomy and opportunities for development or mastery.

Leaders should facilitate access to health resources, training and counseling that can help team members resolve personal and family concerns, resolve conflicts or difficulties, and manage stress, anxiety and depression. When your mind is more at ease and your body healthier, you can perform better and you feel your organization truly cares about you, developing loyalty and rapport.

Rapport: To develop authentic relationships, a leader must genuinely care about their team and needs to frequently demonstrate it through words and deeds. Developing rapport with and among members, requires taking interest in each individual and their interests, concerns, preferences, goals, and values.

By promoting a culture of friendship, care, love, collaboration, and resolution of conflicts, we can, like an integrated family, promote team of teams and collaborative problem solving.

Purpose: I believe it is our natural inclination to seek to be a part of something bigger than ourselves. Leaders can help their people see the significance and meaning of their work in the bigger picture. I believe that leaders can frequently remind their team, through various types of communication, about why their work is important within an exciting vision.

A strong sense of purpose can boost their drive to tackle challenges, feel pride in their work and to feel happier in the long run. By helping individuals align their personal goals with the organizational goals, in shared purpose, team members are more likely to be retained and motivated.

Autonomy: I think it is important to recognize and encourage the development of talent, helping team members have more and more choice over how to do things and to have a portion of their time to develop projects that interest them.

Leaders can give meaningful feedback on progress, create a safe environment to learn, even make mistakes, and provide encouragement to responsibly accrue more responsibility on what and how they spend their time in the organization. Self-direction is a natural human urge, and if developed in accordance to the level of development of the team member, it can result in higher satisfaction and performance.

Growth: I understand that people's happiness and self-worth is associated with their sense of growth versus stagnation. If team members feel that they increase self-mastery and development of skills and knowledge that they value, they will remain happier and motivated.

A leader should take interest in team members' personal goals and encourage them to develop toward fulfilling their potential. By aligning personnel growth with organizational goals, mission, vision, and strategy, they can promote overall success and be accountable to employees and the organization as a whole.

Often, organizations fear investing in people, for fear their investment will benefit a competitor when they leave. Instead, by generously investing in your people, I believe you are more likely to retain your top talent and to create an environment and industry reputation that is attractive to new talent. If you believe in your vision, then even when talent moves on, you see that you are still making a contribution to society and the industry. Your alumni will continue to bring you positive reputation and a sense of pride in the organization.

Environment (atmosphere, culture): As a leader, you can foster an environment of openness, where stakeholders can question, be heard, be creative, make suggestions, take risks feeling safe from discrimination, bullying, shaming, blaming, intimidation where all stakeholders feel safe to express themselves, take moderate risks, make honest mistakes, and grow.

In such an environment, your team can be more comfortable, happier, creative, collaborative and productive. It is easier to harness the potential of the team, when individuals trust their leaders and their coworkers to support them, with a flatter. Leaders who truly listen, act upon recommendations or suggestions, and provide helpful feedback in a kind manner will motivate their team. Collaboration is more likely in such an environment, generating loyalty, trust, innovation and cooperation.

* * * * *

Mohammadreza Bashiri, BSEE, MBA, PE, Ed.D. (CTO) has led teams from a place of genuine care called Conscious Leadership, which he articulates here with his own personal touch. He has a doctorate in Leadership and Change Management from the University of Southern California's Rossier School of Education. Mohammadreza presented this model with Nelson Abreu at the 2019 APQC (American Productivity & Quality Center) PPM (Process and Performance Management) conference in Houston, Texas, USA.
https://www.apquc.org/resource-library/resource-listing/strike-team-case-study-conscious-leadership

Mohammadreza is a proven leader in management and electrical technical education. His extensive hands-on experience as a field engineer and supervisor, makes his courses engaging, informative and highly practical. He has gathered insights on organizational change management and technical education from Malaysia, France, Iran, and North America. His practical experience spans energy storage, apparatus testing, system protection and automation for Renewables; Transmission & Distribution Substations; Commercial/Industrial/Utility Low & Medium Voltage; Petrochem, Oil & Gas. Reza was born in Iran and currently resides in California. He speaks Farsi and English. He is a leader at a major utility in the US and co-founder of Ohm Engineering.

The Tow of the Dow

5. Zero Cost Economics

The following is a transcription of an interview by Nelson Abreu with economist Dr. Farid A. Khavari, PH.D. for Consciousness FM which aired on KPFK Pacifica Radio 90.7 FM in Southern California (January 3, 2017).

SUMMARY: In program 5 of KPFK's Consciousness FM, we talk about a new consciousness leading to new economics with economist Dr. Farid Khavari, author of Zero-Cost Economics. Zero-Cost Economy promotes policies designed to create the maximum economic security for every citizen in a carefree economy. These policies create wealth for everyone by freezing, then reducing, and in some cases eliminating, costs which prevent people from accumulating wealth and living for their purpose and passion, and for their families and communities.

Farid Khavari Bio:
www.zerocosteconomy.com/about_farid_khavari-detailed.html

People are not created to be slaves for some group and work like animals, it's a fact of life. They have come here to live.
DR. FARID KHAVARI

Nelson: Welcome to another session of Consciousness FM. Today we are speaking to Dr. Farid Khavari in Miami. Dr. Farid Khavari has a background in economics and he is advancing a concept called Zero-Cost Economics. Welcome.

Dr. Khavari: Thank you. Good afternoon.

Nelson: Good afternoon. Could you walk our listeners through what the concept is and how you arrived at it?

Dr. Khavari: When I went to Germany to study economics I went to the University of Hamburg. The University of Hamburg was a very conservative university. I had to study there, I did that; and then when I wanted to get my Phd, I had to change 12 or 13 professors, because none of them could understand what I was talking about. Back then I wanted to write about determinants of the oil price policy; I said raising oil prices was a mistake. They could not understand it. So I went to the University of Raymond, a Marxist university, and they welcomed me because of the idea I had. It took me 18 months to get my doctorate degree, and they welcomed me. When I studied both views, I realized there's a big problem in the entire economic concept, and that is cost. And what that means is this: it's designed by nature that everybody when they age, and they end up in their old age, retired, they end up in the poorhouse, no matter how you look at, because the cost keeps rising and the income will eventually stop, especially when you lose your job or you retire. Then you have to live on your fixed income and some savings, if you have any. We're assuming that everybody has a job and is making more money than they are spending. But the fact is, the minute you retire or you lose your job and you have to live on your savings and a fixed income, there will come a time when you outlive your savings and you end up in the poorhouse. You have to downsize and you can only go so long before you end up in the poorhouse. That was a big mistake. This is also the biggest mistake which exists in economic concept. Then there was also the problem that production was based on labor cost and capital. That's another big problem; that's the biggest flaw in all economic concept, because there is an interrelation and interdependence between all economic factors on one side, and then economic textbooks teach us that there is only a correlation between unemployment and inflation, and that by definition means a seesaw economy. By nature it means that we will always have problems, recession and boom, and boom and bust, and that is the problem right there. And then they misinterpret the interrelationship between all economic factors on one hand, and those of technology, raw material, energy, agriculture, and environment on the other hand; and this is the biggest flaw. For instance, you can read any textbook you want or any article you want, and you can find out that they talk about solar energy for instance, but they don't know and they do not distinguish between solar energy that is prosperity-inducing or isn't. That is the problem right there, because they do not understand technology.

Nelson: Let me ask you a question if we can talk about this point in particular. When we look at the world, if we were able to rewrite all the rules, economics or money is supposed to be deposit of value, it's supposed to be an expression of what we value. So when I look at a tree, for example, I can look at it as a living thing, to some extent, really the beginnings of consciousness, and I can respect it a lot. It's not something I can just put a dollar value on based on its timber for example, or even if I look at it in a very objective, material sense, I can think of it as providing shade, providing oxygen, it provides a value that is bigger than whatever I can get once I cut it. By cutting it, I'm taking away from society, but I'm not necessarily giving back. The economic system we have right now doesn't necessarily line up with more ecological, more humanistic values. Can you imagine an economy that can address that?

Dr. Khavari: There's no such economy like that out there. It's based on exploitation. You spoke about money. Money should be used as fertilizer, and I'm not talking Marxism, I'm talking real economics; and the product of that money should be the product that serves the people. We use money with interest and compounded interest to exploit people. By definition we are enslaving the whole society. That's the problem. Money as we know, especially in the United States is created out of thin air. It's created digitally. And then we can do all of these things. We have no economic plan to serve the people, especially to create prosperity, environmentally safe, and sustainable prosperity for all people, and economic security for them. Without economic security there cannot be a prosperous economy. Another problem we have is maximizing profit. Everybody thinks they have to take advantage of other people, especially when you can cheat and exploit people. Why would you do something good? It is much easier to cheat people, exploit people, gouge them, and so on.

Nelson: There is an assumption that greed is good and that that's what drives people. But really, social science shows that that's not exactly true; that we as human beings, as a consciousness are actually naturally driven towards cooperation, towards wanting to develop ourselves. If money wasn't an issue in terms of survival, if that was taken care of somehow, what would drive people after that? It reminds me of Gene Roddenberry in Startrek, they are out there exploring the universe, they're trying to learn, trying to develop, they're helping each other. Of course as you said, if we're not able to provide for our basic needs, it prevents us from knowing ourselves, developing ourselves and helping others more because we're just trying to pay the rent.

Dr. Khavari: If I may inject, not everybody is financially motivated. The musician who plays Mozart, or an inventor who creates or invents something, in my opinion they are more advanced than anybody else especially in the financial sector.

Nelson: It reminds me for example of someone like Jonas Salk, he created a cure that saved millions of lives. He didn't make a penny out of it, but we owe him a great debt.

Dr. Khavari: Trust me, even if you gave him millions of dollars he wouldn't have cared about it. We talk about 1% millionaires who are rich and super rich. But 99% of people like you and me work. And they are interested in having a nice family, a nice life, and be able to continue that life as long as they live. This is where we come into the picture, and we should take care of that. Not everybody's greedy. By the way, what could you do with 100 billion dollars more than you could do with 50 billion dollars or 100 million dollars? Why would we want 100 billion dollars?

Nelson: So if we don't like Communism, Marxism, where everybody is reduced to a very low common denominator, or we don't like vulture Capitalism that by default tries to fool people into thinking that if you work hard you will necessarily make more money, but instead is actually rigged to benefit very few people; what is the alternative?

Dr. Khavari: A Zero-Cost Economy. What that means is we have to first put people into a position where they have a house, they have energy, a vehicle to move around in, a job, and so on. Once that happens we have to create a system where we could achieve all these things in a short period of time. That means we have to eliminate reoccurring costs and social costs because reoccurring costs comes from the drive for reoccurring income and revenue. That reoccurring revenue and income for some companies is a reoccurring cost for a lot of people. The fact is the people cannot get a raise and adjust their salary to the rising cost, so they have to live on their savings. This is the big problem right there. First we have to implement all measures that decrease the cost, reduce the cost, and wherever possible eliminate the cost; that is the basics of the concept of Zero-Cost Economy. We talk about the solar energy system. Environmentally there's no problem. But there are many problems between the two systems: decentralized solar system and centralized solar system. A decentralized solar system that you and I have on our house, is a prosperity-inducing energy system. But if we get a centralized solar system like a power company with a big huge solar plant somewhere, it is environmentally fine, but it doesn't induce prosperity for the people because you keep paying the electric rates for it.

Nelson: I suppose what it comes down to is who owns the means of production. It could be a large utility scale project, but maybe if it was cooperatively owned by people it would still work out in a different way as opposed to being corporately owned by very few people.

Dr. Khavari: First we have to get rid of the corruption in government. We have to take politics, parties, and money out of our political system.

Nelson: People are able to move away from the system by cooperatively owning the means of production with their neighbors, with their family, with their coworkers; then by having more prosperity at least they can also have a voice. Ideally we want to make it more about issues rather than parties and passion points. Of course we know this but to implement it, to reach there, takes a movement. People have to really campaign behind those principles. We hope to see more and more of that. Going back to your system, if there is no or little cost, in one sense that's great, because I can carry on my life with very few costs to me. But we have a system based on money. So if there are few costs, it also means that when I provide a service I can't charge a big fee. It's like saying a money-free society. How can you have a society with little cost and therefore little salaries. We have to rethink the whole thing. How would that work?

Dr. Khavari: Let's assume we get a solar system on your house. The minute we put that solar system on your house, it increases the cost; after 4-5 years when it's payed for, the energy cost becomes zero, because that system lasts 20-30 years. I was in manufacturing, I have a system I put on my house in 1980. It's still functioning. Once you do that and that's what we have to increase productivity in, and in economic textbooks you don't find any definition for productivity in the service sector, you don't see it. We have to increase productivity in the service sector, and by doing that we could cut the healthcare cost about 50%.

Nelson: I like the idea of changing the way we think about ourselves and others and our purpose here, and building an economy that works for our development, rather than enslaving us and moving us away from our nature and purpose. If you can help make that happen, we all have that gratitude to you, and at least we thank you for trying. I invite our listeners to learn more about the zero cost economy and I thank you for your time.

* * * * *

JOHN MAYNARD KEYNES in his 1930 letter essay Economic possibilities for our grandchildren wrote about the power of compound interest and usury (charging interest on debt money). "..the exaction of usury is a misdemeanour, and the love of money is detestable". He imagined at the beginning of the Great Depression "an age of leisure and abundance....to return to some of the most sure and certain principles of religion and traditional. We shall once more value ends above means and prefer the good to the useful. We shall honour those who can teach us how to pluck the hour and the day virtuously and well, the delightful people who are capable of taking direct enjoyment in things, the lilies of the field who toil not, neither do they spin."

The key is to somehow find a way of tackling rent-seeking, crony capitalism, and corruption - legal and illegal - and build fairer, more equal society without compromising innovation or entrepreneurship.
ANGUS DEATON

Some people say we have this inequality because some people have been contributing much more to our society, and so it's fair that they get more. But then you look at the people who are at the top, and you

realize they're not the people who have transformed our economy, our society.
JOSEPH E. STIGLITZ

It is well enough that people of the nation do not understand our banking and monetary system, for if they did, I believe there would be a revolution before tomorrow morning.
HENRY FORD

6. Smart Cities, Healthy Cities: City as a Health Ecosystem

Malcolm Gladwell's *Outliers* argues that, though individual actions are crucial, success has much to do with the genetics and environment. If you have not read this interesting work, you can read an excerpt (first chapter) in the NY Times website, which praises the work of Dr. Stewart Wolf. Upon realizing the low incidence of heart disease of a community of Italian immigrants, Dr. Wolf eventually discovered that aspects of their community were the biggest contributing factors, rather than genetics, diet, exercise and other commonly discussed health parameters. When we think of Smart Cities, we cannot avoid thinking about how healthy they are to live in. Inevitably, we must consider the objective environment. For instance, how healthy is the air, the water, the available food choice? Does the city facilitate physical fitness or a more sedentary lifestyle? However, Dr. Wolf's work suggests the more intangible, subjective or internal life of citizens can lead to objectively different health outcomes, as well. In other words, cities are not just places to sleep, eat, commute, work but also places to contemplate, to learn, to commune, and to play. No city that overlooks the quality of the subjective reality of its citizens, their happiness, and the intersubjective aspect, their sense of connectedness with those around them, can call itself a smart city.

A smart city needs to be run by leaders who understand this and have the integrity to make decisions that uplift the work force. When workers are afraid to speak or make mistakes, they are not as productive, cooperative nor creative. Leaders who genuinely care and create safe and supportive environments promote collaborative, respectful and inclusive behaviors. Access to a livable wage and good benefits along with resources like mindfulness can reduce stress, anxiety and even pain. With an atmosphere free of harassment and intimidation, a diverse and vibrant team can take more creative risks essential for the new economy. Happier workers produce more, get sick less often, and can improve communication with customers and collaboration with coworkers.

When a person works in a toxic work place or is in poverty, the brain's limbic system is constantly sending fear and stress messages to the prefrontal cortex, which can overload the ability to solve problems, set goals, and complete tasks in the most effective ways. When brain capacity is used up on these worries and fears, there simply isn't as much bandwidth for other things. This sets back development for families, companies and entire countries. On the other hand, understanding how the human mind works and how it is possible to ethically influence and help others can lead to better workplaces and a path out of poverty for many.

Does your company promote mental fitness? Emotional resilience and mindfulness along with a genuine effort by leadership to create a safe and caring environment can define success in the 21st century. Happier employees can translate to significant financial benefits as well.

A study by the North American insurance company Aetna found mindfulness practices cut stress levels by 1/3. It also reduced healthcare costs by US $2,000 per year per employee with just one 1 hr/week of practice.

Insurance companies around the world are actively promoting mindfulness to reduce illness and injury. It lowers healthcare costs for companies and raises insurance company profits. Additionally, Aetna workers regained an average of 62 minutes of productivity per week.

For instance, for an organization with 9,000 employees, this would translate to US $18 million per year in healthcare cost savings and 483,600 hours of recovered productivity – at US $100 per hour loaded cost, this translates to over US $48M annually. Besides the US $66 million dollars per year in direct savings, there is improved employee and customer happiness and new improvements and innovations resulting from this improved condition.

Most workplace injuries result from inattention, which can improve with mindfulness practices. A reduction in injuries, outages, fines, lawsuits and damaged equipment due to error mitigation can also make a significant impact.

Mindfulness practices and healthy altered states deliver measurable benefits including: reduced stress, lower blood pressure, improved attention and memory, reduced depression, anxiety, and pain. Mindfulness correlated with reduced amygdala density and lower activity during stress response; reduced pain levels (~40% with 30 min training) which is important amidst the opioid crisis; reduced inflammation, which correlates with many diseases.

Positive emotions, improved emotional intelligence and resilience will also create a more pleasant and creative workplace. With improved work-place well-being comes improved staff retention, communication, collaboration, creative problem-solving (insight), and customer service.

Mindfulness can significantly reduce work-related injuries; reduce work-place errors and associated injuries, deaths, damage, service interruptions, rework, and reduce sick days.

Helping workers feel better is the right thing to do – and it helps them perform better. In the 21st century economy of artificial intelligence and robotics, creativity and human warmth are even more valuable. Mindfulness training and conscious tech can promote both.

The Tow of the Dow

7. Vitalism: Beyond Capitalism & Communism
A Vision for Portugal

The 21st century will belong to those who clearly articulate their values and strive to be consistent with them. Its virtue will help to develop, attract and retain ethical and creative individuals and communities in a world with ever-increasing technological automation and inequality and fewer jobs.

We must go beyond the tired ideas of the socialists and neoliberals, from "wealth for the rich raises all boats," "job creation" to the "redistribution" of the wealth of some ultra-rich.

Of course, both the usual alternating parties in power have some good ideas, but have proven to be incompetent. Civil society is forward-looking, diverse and competent and is striving for more direct involvement in governance and reducing dependence on disillusioning representatives.

We do not want to take the wealth of the entrepreneur and redistribute to the masses. We do not want a society of savage slave capitalism in underdeveloped nations and workers tied to hourly servitude or unemployment, surrendered to the materialistic paradigm. We do not want a communist dystopia where the state is a giant, corrupt corporation with ultra-rich plutocrats and masses of powerless people who are just surviving with their extinguished individual flame. So, in the end, what do we want?

The Portuguese people have a proud history of innovation, discovery, entrepreneurship, courage, culture and social awareness. We embrace our common humanity, our international and European ties, but we must regain our civilization, our sovereignty and once again we will be leaders. The new oceans to be faced are those of the human mind and spirit, from which comes all innovation, culture, engineering, science, ethics, courage, and perseverance.

Let's show the world that Portugal is not a small country with little minds. Portugal has immense natural resources - sunshine, a beautiful coast, economic, cultural, historical resources, overseas ties, an immense exclusive economic zone in the Atlantic, and rich spiritual traditions. Its highest principles can show the world that knowledge-based civilization and ethics are a thriving enlightened force: democratic, peaceful and courageous for the greater good, while protecting individual freedom and cultivating the realization of potential: the potential of individuals, communities, places and ideas.

Visualize this condition: Individuals and groups are rewarded for collaboration and wealth creation through workers who are also owners of their cooperative enterprises; imagine positive sovereign investment, savings and insurance instruments.

The new wealth is multiplied with investments in new small and medium enterprises. Workers are co-owners in many of these companies, and can accumulate enough to pursue their own interests and passions - their activities can enrich culture, innovation, new economic engines, and collective welfare.

When some of our countrymen are experiencing health or other difficulties, their well-being is guaranteed by access to the most basic needs: minimum income, shelter, public services and education. The same benefit is available as a safety net for the citizen or resident who wants to create a smart business venture or is displaced by changes in his industry.

What we pejoratively call unemployment is in fact the freedom from slavery and exploitation that most people have sought. Few of us would be content with a near-poverty subsistence level. Freedom from the struggle for mere survival frees us to contribute to society, to volunteer for positive causes, to follow our creative passions, and to develop as human beings.

This collective facilitation of wealth creation can replace state-sponsored permanent poverty for populist vote manipulation or the self-enrichment of professional politicians and their special interests to the detriment of the majority.

What prevents the nation from fulfilling its natural destiny as an enlightened society? Apathy or discouragement in the face of the oligarchy is a big part. If we are cynical and believe that nothing can be done, our future and the future of our descendants will be a self-fulfilling prophecy. If we are coherent and educate the next generations and defend their future together, democracy will become healthier.

We allow a few people drunk with power to put themselves in front of millions of Portuguese citizens. The Portuguese are perfectly capable of governing without professional politicians, who often represent the interests of corrupt elites. All citizens need are modern versions of democratic instruments from Ancient Greece, the origin of democracy, in order to make informed decisions:

1) freedom of the press and freedom of expression
2) deliberation and consultation of experts in relevant areas representing a range of points from public view
3) more direct democracy is amplified through methods such as the draw, local assemblies, civic budget approvals, and facilitation of citizen initiatives, and / or deliberative polling.
4) short deadlines and stronger limitation on number of terms (none or few professional, permanent political class). The number and duration of political office mandates should be highly limited.
5) liability for negligence or corruption (public dishonor, imprisonment, fines or lengthy, compulsory community service)
6) greater local and regional control of budgets with strong ethics oversight and smaller national bureaucracies (more autonomy and experimentation according to common principles and laws)

In an era where production costs are getting lower with automation, there is less and less traditional work. Instead of creating precariousness and abandonment, we can use technology to free more and more people so that they can create, collaborate, and contribute to the community. Creativity, culture, human warmth cannot be replaced by machines.

Portugal should be known throughout the world as a nation of great spirit that collectively harnesses individual talents, preserves and offers an age-old cultural and sensory experience with personal touch, and invests in its ideas for philosophy, science, technology and arts, eventually developing, attracting and retaining the best minds and hearts in the country and from around the world.

We can choose to be the new Athens, the new Sagres, the new Cape Canaveral... in partnership with the Lusophone world and the Mediterranean.

There is no wealth but life. Life, including all its powers of love, of joy, and of admiration. That country is the richest which nourishes the greatest number of noble and happy human beings; that man is richest who, having perfected the functions of his own life to the utmost, has also the widest helpful influence, both personal, and by means of his possessions, over the lives of others.
JOHN RUSKIN (1819-1900) (Unto this Last)

8. What Steve Jobs Understood About Consciousness and Design

Accounts of the development of the personal computing revolution focus on technology or business, but early insiders and readers of *What the Dormouse Said: How the Sixties Counter culture Shaped the Personal Computer Industry* by John Markoff know about the counter-culture and consciousness expansion behind the first PCs: a group of visionaries set out to turn computers into a means for freeing minds and information.

Many of the pioneers were inspired through cognitive shifts experienced through mindfulness practices and, often, drugs (which we do not endorse). Steve Jobs, for instance, reportedly said that taking the psychedelic drug LSD was a profound experience ("one of the two or three most important things I have done in my life"). While in college, Jobs shared an interest in consciousness and spirituality with friends with whom he would discuss experiences and books related to the concept of chi.

Steve Jobs said the following: "Taking LSD was a profound experience, one of the most important things in my life. LSD shows you that there's another side to the coin, and you can't remember it when it wears off, but you know it. It reinforced my sense of what was important—creating great things instead of making money, putting things back into the stream of history and of human consciousness as much as I could."

Such transpersonal experiences, which may be achieved drug-free through techniques and technologies employed at I-ACT, often lead experiencers to a paradigm shift. Instead of viewing themselves as completely separate intelligent apes, they tend to conclude that the physical world, including other humans, animals, trees and even what is human-designed, are all connected as extensions of consciousness. What we design is a reflection of our inner essence and, therefore, can play an important role, complementary to science in the understanding of reality.

Part of Jobs' genius may be the realization that people appreciate the "luxuriousness" of experience even more than accumulating things: humans are attracted to the internal, subjective, irreducible delight of good design and are highly responsive to beauty. Color, taste, love, pleasure, curiosity, motivation, creativity, humor, beauty and other subjective experiences may have physical correlates, but our experience is not physical per se. Our most intimate reality, that which we know the best and often value the most, may not be easily measured.

Take color for instance. Physics, engineering and architecture may approach color in a different way (for instance, as more than a poetic statement; we challenge anyone to successfully argue otherwise. Another example: frequency can be a signal or an aesthetic element). We may judge it in purely objective terms, but our judgment of color, spaces, forms, our experience of the built environment (or of anything in our physical reality for that matter) is something inherently internal. The progression is to view everything we consider "solid" or "physical" as an extension of ourselves -- including the designed environment, as posited by our co-founder and architectural designer Manori Sumanasinghe, who studies the interplay between consciousness and design, architecture and urban design.

When we admire a beautiful sunset, the sense of beauty exists only in our microcosm. However, sight (of the form and color of the sun), though facilitated by physics and physiology, is experienced internally, as is the warmth we feel on our skin. The sun is particularly interesting, as the light that reaches our eyes and skin has had to travel for minutes and then processed for milliseconds before it comes to our visual and tactile awareness. However, if we were concentrated on driving a vehicle, our eyes might receive the same light energy but not be consciously aware of the sunset, let alone awed by its perceived beauty. How do we know the sun exists? We base the conclusion that it exists in some objective way on the consensus that others also perceived it and share similar, though, not identical, experiences of the sun. This means that we base our perception of an objective reality on subjective observation.

In fact, there is no way to prove that something exists independently of observers, as our judgment of reality relies on some form of observation or measurement, which is itself ultimately internal. This view was argued by some of the greatest minds in history, like physicists Bohr, Schoedinger, Pauli, and Wigner. Swiss consciousness scholar and physicist Massimiliano Sassolli de Bianchi posits that particles studied by physicists simply do not exist. They "appear" into existence when we make a measurement. In other words, they are an interpretation of our interaction with nano-scale reality. There is no evidence that they exist as real, corpuscular entities beyond concepts that are independent of the observational process.

Everything we consider physical, including the natural and built environment, and our own bodies is composed of this same energy and is, therefore, intimately tied to our microcosm. External reality makes no sense without internal reality, each one giving meaning to the other, acting as two complementary aspects of one reality. The surround, the theater is inside us, it is us, and we are therefore not limited, localized entities.

Jobs and others understood that the internal experience takes precedence. Certainly, a high standard of quality, excellent customer service and effectiveness of a product are highly relevant, but the consumer's microcosm also responds to the fact that someone else takes the time and effort to feed his or her senses: whether it is a beautiful meal, "coffee art," humor in an otherwise expressionless moment, or the spectacular shell of a public building. In other words, design can be considered a way to honor the fact that we are more than our bodies, for it recognizes our intangible dimensions that separate us from machines and most pre-human animals.

Indeed, we see that as affluence and education frees more individuals from the struggle for survival, more people can attend to their higher needs per Maslow's hierarchy of needs. With an abundance of choices for products in the market, success favors those who employ design principles, make products, places and services that not only address an objective problem in Space and Time, but also consider the Subjective experience of the individual. There is increased attention to the internal aspect of humans that responds to comfort, user-friendliness, taste, aesthetics, sense of purpose, belonging, status.

Art and design is increasingly part of our everyday lives, starting with the unique ways we manifest ourselves, like the way we speak, dress, and solve personal or career challenges. We also see that along with an increased level of automation and analysis performed by computers, comes a special relevance and competitive advantage for human intuition, creativity, and – yes – artistic expression, as can be witnessed by the pervasiveness of design. It is no longer enough to produce a pen, a computer, a vehicle, a house or a chair that works well.

We also find art and design being used in the service of non-commercial causes: consider, for instance, how Art has been used to better convey important ideas such as Liberty, Human Rights, and Ecology. Story-telling through creative expression such as poetry, drama, song, painting, sculpture, and literature - and increasingly viral YouTube videos - is often more effective for (or an important part of) educating and effecting change, when compared to a scientific paper or a prosaic lecture.

Jobs had his flaws and we can question the deleterious aspects of today's manufacturing and unhealthy effects of looking more at screens than the world and people around us. However, Jobs clearly sought to "invent" the future, rather than survey what people thought they wanted based on what is already prevalent within their current paradigms. He understood the world of consciousness as something one could draw from and also contribute to. Consciousness practices may help us tune in to and develop different dimensions of consciousness.

With the world of the subjective playing an increasingly important role for social and commercial enterprise, what can be done to optimize our creative output?

Neuma Being is an organization that works with innovators in the sciences, engineering, architecture and design, film and other arts, problem-solvers and creatives who seek their next breakthrough insight. We also help individuals who seek to remain healthy and vital through their demanding lifestyle. We draw on a trusted network of experts in consciousness development and wellness and leading-edge techniques and technology to help individuals and organizations worldwide.

The Tao of the Dow

9. Internal Reality: Emerging Conscious Tech

This chapter is an interview by Suma Gowda of Wagner Alegretti and Nelson Abreu on January 6, 2020. Wagner Alegretti is co-founder of IAC & I-ACT. Nelson Abreu is CTO of Neumascape Studio and Neuma Being, home of the Neuma Mind Spa & Showroom.

Suma: The first question I wanted to start with was some of the practical applications of these transformative experiences. How can people use this in everyday life?

Wagner: Perhaps Nelson you can start.

Nelson: Sure. For a long time I've had the privilege to be mentored by people like Wagner. Sometimes you read books and you think I really wish I had a chance to meet this person, and I've had this privilege to meet people like Wagner, and know him by first name. It's really, really amazing to me. Just listening to you guys talk earlier, reminded me that it's really special. One thing is that we have been trying to communicate to people all over the world the value of an out-of-body experience, energy, and what we found is that there's a niche group of people who are ready to take the red pill like in the matrix, and expand their horizons, that's wonderful, and we're there for them as an organization. However, I also had another mentor, who I didn't get to spend as much time with, Robert Jahn from the Princeton PEAR Laboratory, and Brenda Dunne, who I'm still very happy to be in touch with. Bob, shortly after receiving a lifetime achievement award from IAC, he passed away recently, but he left a rallying cry for us, which was to take all these experiences and research that has been done, and find a way to connect this work to people's everyday life. Your question really goes to that. How can we go to where people are, meet them where they are? Maybe there are a lot of people right now who don't think it's relevant to have an out-of-body experience, or to learn about energy, because they don't see the connection. So how can we help bridge that gap, make it more pragmatic.

Maybe after they see pragmatic uses, it will awaken an interest to go deeper. And then they can take advantage of things like Consciousness Development program at IAC and so on. But we notice that a lot of people aren't quite at that moment in their lives. So as far as practical applications are concerned, I think sometimes people forget the very basic, which is you get so caught up in trying to persuade people that this experience has a particular nature, if it's real or not real, you forget that this is actually a set of very exciting and enjoyable experiences. I really enjoy having out-of-body experiences.

Wagner: It's an exploration.

Nelson: How much do people pay for a VR experience? Right? This is free. It's in your mind, it's in your brain, it's maybe beyond your brain. It doesn't even matter. It's within your reach. I think the first application is frankly, free and amazing entertainment. It's just something enjoyable. How many inventions came out of dreams? But that was not a real experience…who cares? There's an amazing new invention, scientific work, piece of artwork that came out of that experience. So how many good ideas for a scientific breakthrough could come out of an out-of-body experience? How many beautiful works of art, how many engineering marvels could happen? They have already happened in the past, but if you make it more accessible, then more of them will happen. So maybe instead of always trying to talk about the experience in terms of what is it's ultimate nature, sometimes to certain groups of people, which is I think is most people, it might be more productive to talk to them in terms of how it can be useful and interesting for them in their everyday life, starting with the most basic things.

Wagner: So when we talk about these basic things, we can go back to that pyramid Maslow's basic needs. All this knowledge can help people in almost all those levels there because there is even a kind of spiritual level, need, more at the tip, of that pyramid; but even at the level where they put very physical needs for food and protection, people do not understand that energy is a basic need we have, it's the quality of our environment. So one of the things that we have been discussing a lot, not only us but also our colleagues, is a larger and deeper understanding of well-being. Well-being comes from some things outside, it's very difficult for a person to say he or she has well-being when a person is hungry. But even when people have everything in life, sometimes they don't have well-being enough, good enough, so what is missing there? What is it that we need in life?

For instance one big thing in well-being is having a purpose. When a person doesn't have a purpose, basically other things are irrelevant. Some people commit suicide because they don't have a purpose. Some people die young or younger than they should because they don't have a purpose. I was telling in a recent course about an experience I had with a person, dead now, but at the time he was among the oldest people on this planet. His name is Alexander Image. He's a person you can Google, a very influential person. When we met him, he was 106 years old. He died being 112 years old. At the time he was the oldest man on this planet. Then after many discussions about ectoplasm, the paranormal, his experiences, so many different things, in fact he donated part of his personal library to IAC. But then in one of the moments there in his apartment in New York, I asked him, "Look, what can you tell us about longevity, because you are the real deal, you are not a very young doctor, talking about longevity." He said a lot of things that we know about exercising and diet, and this and that, and then he said, "No, look, I'm forgetting the most important thing, always have a purpose in your life, otherwise, you'll die." He said, "How many of my friends, colleagues, and relatives, they died, being younger than me, because they just ran out of challenges, things to do."

So when we think about consciousness exploration, evolution, it gives a purpose, a different kind of well-being, introduces energy, ethics. When you think that you can have such an important role in people's evolution, even with of course your channel. You do a very beautiful, big thing here, because this is what people need the most. Information with quality, with depth. Because most of the things we see nowadays, not all of course, it would be unfair to say that, but so many things are so superficial, my goodness, that don't make any difference. We have so many different needs, we have to update that pyramid.

Nelson: That's right. Continuing in that vein of pragmatic applications, I never imagined I would sit with managers in companies that are not at all interested to hear about having OBEs in other planets (laugh), but what they are interested in is productivity, reducing sick days, reducing injuries, improving creativity and innovation, and improving the overall psychological safety of the workplace, these are all things that can be aided through mindfulness practices, mindfulness practices that can include energy mindfulness, energy practices. I actually found myself where they were asking me "Can you teach us something." I gave them a very brief taste of vibrational state-related type techniques. They were doing the techniques not to have some kind of spiritual breakthrough, but to deal with the stresses of the workplace, to have more resilience, to have more resistance in terms of fatigue, to make fewer mistakes, to get through the day more productively, and to have a little thicker skin, paraskin, in terms of dealing with problems with colleagues, customers, difficult pressures of deadlines and so on. The fact that you could have less stress really means less inflammation, less pain, fewer sick days, or less proneness to certain illnesses, just overall better well-being. Feel good when you come to work and feel good when you get home, and be more pleasant to other people. Other people will like you more too, your customers, your colleagues, your family.

These are basic applications that your traditional mindfulness techniques can help with, even the kind of techniques that IAC teaches with energy. In my line of work I get paid to work with a different kind of energy, the kind that powers houses and factories, and I work around thousands of volts. One mistake could cause an outage for the whole southern California, or it could be my last mistake in this physical body, or someone else's which is in some ways worse, because then you live with the guilt of getting someone else hurt. It's very important to have attention and not get too wound up under stress, under pressure. So when something doesn't go according to the plan, that's when you need it the most, a calm, collected mind. And I find myself even as an instinct, I start applying these energy techniques. I don't even have to think of it. It's just second nature to me now. It helps me tremendously. Even in an office environment when things are tense, people sometimes have told me, what's wrong with you, you're the only person smiling here. It's hard to stay mad when we're around you. We start to wonder, is there something wrong with us? Maybe. Maybe we need to work on our culture here, on our environment. Sometimes just you being you, or a slightly better version of you, because you are applying these techniques, can be infectious, can affect others. It is a big part of communication, I think Wagner can speak to this, communication is mostly non-verbal, and non-verbal doesn't just mean how you dress, how you move, it's about energy. You're the energy expert so I'll let you tackle that one.

Wagner: Yes, because many times we see people who are so called charismatic, and we know that charisma comes from energy. Of course with more energy there is going to be more influence. Not always positive, of course that's why we always have to combine it with ethics; because Hitler was a very charismatic leader, very influential, could communicate really well, but we know the results of that. How can we have this power of presence, being there really as a tool for evolution, and being very conscious of the responsibility for that. So as Nelson was saying, giving some examples of application of many of these ideas, energy, in a professional environment, but can you imagine for instance in schools, if kids could start today relaxing, doing some simple form of mindfulness, and then absorbing energy, I think many of them would be able to pay more attention for longer, enjoying the thing, being more creative, absorbing more information, and think about that in a hospital, one of the most stressful environments we can think of, even think for instance about energy being applied in sports performance, so any aspect of our life can be improved by using energy.

Nelson: I was surprised, the soccer player who scored the winning goal for the Portuguese national team, to win the European championship, it was into overtime, the star player was injured early in the game, it was zero-zero, nobody expected this guy who had just been underwhelming, because he had such potential, but he had never really quite lived up to it, but they put him in, because he is a very strong man, it was a burst of energy at the end. He just did this most magical goal, and people were wowed, he really for first time shown, as he should. When they were interviewing him, he said, "I want to dedicate this achievement to my mental coach." I did a double take. People are getting into this. The Miami Heat, when they were at their height, they were doing meditation classes. People are learning this secret.

Also, the research that we're learning is that when you have a better vegus nerve, the vegus nerve, the biggest nerve that we have that runs the length of our body, has to do with fight or flight, and has a lot to do with the level of inflammation in our body, if you have better vegus nerve tone, you're able to learn better. If there's more vegus nerve stimulation at the moment of learning, there's better retention, and better neural plasticity, the ability to change our previous ways of thinking and so on. What can effect vegus tone? There are technologies like pulses of light, electricity, ultrasound, but these practices are doing it without any wires, as well. So definitely learning, focus, creativity, it's all there. These are things that everyone wants. But I suspect, really part of our mission in the next stage of our work, is to normalize these things. Just like yoga. When you thought about yoga back in the day it was probably an Indian man in a cloth, doing their thing. No women, it was mostly men. And there was definitely no western men either. It was a very specific culture. But nowadays you see women, some men as well, wearing Lululemon, or whatever, and it's just a thing you do. Jogging…yoga. Some people would say that's a watered down yoga, and it's not what it used to be, that's true, no question, but by normalizing it, at least now more people can learn about the original yoga. I spoke to Dean Radin some time ago about this, and having this discussion, what he said was, that's true, maybe yoga of today is some kind of kinesthetic alternative, but if you go to a yoga conference and you ask the question, how many of you have felt energy, how many of you have had an out-of-body experience, a lot of hands are going to raise up. Which means, yes, maybe we do need a watered down version, not to the point of selling out, but just to make it as an entryway. Again, it's this theme of meeting people where they are today, to help them eventually get to where we feel they could really have a spiritual, ethical breakthrough. But you have to start somewhere.

Wagner: If I may, you mentioned in the beginning, technology. I would like to bring something to the discussion. Many times people think technology is only machines, devices, electronics. Technology is more than that, a technique, a way of doing something is technology. A material developed is technology, this is technology, a shoe, this is technology. So when we mention technology, people think only of the high end technology, but how many things could we do in a different way. So when we think of applying a particular technique, using energy, like VELO, moving energy, increasing the speed; by the way, if you Google VELO/Nanci Trivellato, there is in fact a course, a training for that (just to be accessible to your audience). But in a way, that is a form of technology. I went to some big companies in Brazil when I was there to give lectures or workshops, and one of the things the leaders there many times brought to me was how some particular conditions or states were in fact contagious, infectious to people. Laziness is infectious, if you have one or two the whole thing is going to come down. Depression, some people brought the following case: a person comes here on a Monday after some problems over the weekend, the whole team goes down. Anxiety, and so many other things. This guy was asking me, "Is there anything we can do to shield people, to avoid this kind of contamination, what can we do to improve?" What I did many times was to try to teach people technology, start the day absorbing energy, doing VELO. Sometimes some companies, for instance in Japan, start with a physical exercise in a group, everyone in the morning with some movement. Not in a forced way, but I think a lot of companies could start with 10 minutes of mindfulness, some energy work, and everything could be better. Perhaps it's not the solution for everything of course, nothing is easy, but it could be big tool there.

Nelson: An insurance company calculated that 5 minutes of mindfulness every day translates approximately to $2,000 per person per year, in savings, in terms of insurance costs, and improved productivity.

Wagner: Creativity, problem-solving skills.

Nelson: Also, in a bigger way, today's economy (earlier you were talking about AI) a lot of the jobs are going to be automated. This can be a threat. It can be destabilizing. But on the other hand, it can be liberating. It will free people up to do what people do best: rapport, understanding people, showing affection, showing empathy, creating new things, innovation, and this is something that will make what we are talking about here even more relevant. Mastering energy is a process of providing better customer support, dealing with difficult customers so that you don't get burned out. That's a big thing that could go a long, long way. Having that next breakthrough idea could come through a lucid dream, through an out-of-body experience, through meditation, through the hypnagogic period between awake and asleep. I think companies understand this. That's why they're buying sleep pods and nap pods. They have massage therapists on the payroll because they need these things not to burn out because they work so many hours, but also to be creative. It goes hand in hand. I think we'll see more and more of this.

Wagner: A good example, at least in my case, because I do these one-on-one sessions. The biggest largest group would be psychologists, clinical psychologists who are exhausted, drained. It's not only by the energy per se, but being so contaminated by so many sessions with so many people, so many problems, they don't know how to cleanse that condition. This has been the most common in terms of demographics. Everyone dealing directly with the public, medical doctors, masseurs, they tend to have this kind of energy assimilation. Many don't know how to get rid of it. After a while the person is really contaminated, is in dissonance with health, with mental condition, with the emotional stability of the person. Some of these energy techniques can help the person that way.

Nelson: In a bigger sense also, earlier we were talking about how many crises we're facing in the world; and we're not really missing money, technology, it's all there. It's available. And if it's not available, humans have enough ingenuity to make it happen. We can land people on the moon, we can do whatever we need to improve the world. But what Wagner was saying earlier is we have an ethical crisis. We have lack of will, lack of imagination. There is a phenomenon that is very interesting to me, that is what astronauts who go into outer space experience, they call it the Overview Effect. They go into outer space, they're already very smart, and educated, planetary scientists, physicists, these are very smart cookies. They are there, men and women, looking down at the earth. They already know all the science that's pertinent, that's available, but now there's a visceral understanding, it's different. They have a visceral understanding that the earth is already floating through space. We are already in space. This earth and the 7 billion plus people living in it are only protected by only a thin layer of the atmosphere and the magnetic field of the earth, how fragile life is, how there's no borders, and we're one big family, bickering family but we are one big family, and they come back changed forever. Now they have a planetary identity. They are man, woman, Indian, American, whatever, but first and foremost a planetary member. There's a parallel with this when I had my first out-of-body experiences, I got a similar shift. I thought, I'm part of a cosmic family first and foremost, before being male, or any sort of ethnicity or skin color. I'm a consciousness first. You don't go through life the same way. I don't see any better application than that. What the world needs is people who are more inspired. Just having these experiences undeniable makes people for the most part, not in all cases, but in most cases, more ecological, more fraternal, more inspired to do something in the world. To me, that's the ultimate application of what we do.

Wagner: I was going to change to another subject, because we mentioned during our break, that even our relation with pets/animals change when you can feel energy, when you can apply energy. Not all, but many pets are very sensitive. They sense their guardian, we don't say owner. We can interact with them with energy. I had so many interesting experiences when I was using, testing, playing a little with energy. The animals could sense, sometimes I'd get this distracted look through the window, you send energy and the cat suddenly... what was that? Imagine how much more we could understand these beings. In the campus in IAC Portugal we have a 3-house we call the 5 labs, 5 different plants, 5 energy labs. When people go there they stay in this little house, very comfortable, very cozy, they relax and try to commune and connect with the energies of the plant, the auric field. When they succeed, when they are there and they can really make this auric energy coupling with the tree, they sense the tree in a completely different way. They end up respecting the green life more, the trees, and the plants. Many times people even feel the consciousness of the tree. Because when we see trees, we're usually a little blind to them. In fact there is an expression called 'green blindness' because people don't see the trees. We think they're just something to make the place more beautiful, or for wood, but when you can really feel that there's a mind, simpler perhaps, but a kind of a mind there, and people say "I will never be able to see or think of trees in the same way again." They sense the tree, the connections with everything else, and I think people need that kind of experience to be able to feel responsible. I want to protect that being. It's not just something you go out there and prune the branches, whatever you allow to die, because you care, it is important for you. Think of this expansion of our energy perception to create a different kind of empathy towards the environment. Because really there's a species disappearing and dying, but people don't feel empathy for that. Trees are dying, by the way, trees are dying by the millions, it's not just because trees are being burned, or being cut, it's by diseases, and everything else, so what's going on? With this heightened sense of awareness perception, I think we can have a higher well-being, as we discussed before. There's no well-being for us without mother nature around us, it's impossible.

Nelson: With that, you have a shift in consciousness from 'I am alone in a competitive world' to 'I am an interdependent being part of an ecology.' That shifts everything. Talk about applications. How does the economic system change when you understand that? How does something that is an externality become now part of that system? How do we account for that? There's a Portuguese economist who's developing and promoting a new model, that's basically treating the earth as a condominium. I think that's pretty brilliant. So you pay your condo fee to take advantage of the common amenities. It's not for free. It has to be maintained. If you go and destroy part of the condominium, you're accountable for it because you're affecting your fellow neighbors. I think we will see with more imagination, which also stems from consciousness, from being, we will develop better models to be in a workplace, to collaborate, better models to exist in better harmony with other beings on earth as well, and other human beings in general as well.

Wagner: I think this goes so deep because even some of the ethical principles, perhaps not so ethical, but mottoes for people like 'Go forth and multiply' - very important for a lot of people. This was reasonable 5,000 years ago. But nowadays, I don't know if that's still applicable. How many people would be able to go back to the foundations of their values and beliefs, to redo, rethink, and reanalyze some things. I'm not saying that everything has to be thrown out the window, of course not. But some of these things have to be tweaked.

Nelson: A software update.

Wagner: Exactly, some little patches here and there. So when some people say let us save the planet, I think there's something wrong because the planet as an astronomical, astrophysical thing, doesn't need any saving. Our biosphere, this particular set of conditions, temperature, rain, and everything, this is what has to be saved, because perhaps outside of these conditions our species is not viable here. That's the thing. Even at some of these events I go to dealing with ecology, when they're open to this more of a multidimensional point of view, I was invited by a few of them, so I asked the people, "Even if you are very selfish, but if you believe in reincarnation, what kind of planet are you going to find yourself in, in the next life when you reincarnate? What is the kind of planet you would prefer? Because it's up to us." I think that's a very good application of karma, if we think of karma as action/reaction, consequences for our actions or inactions, so if people believe in being born again, next life, let us see what kind of earth we're going to inherit next time we come here. I think that's important.

Suma: Are there are some good pointers and applications for transformative experiences? What kinds of organizations come to IAC? What are some of the things they ask for at IAC?

Wagner: As Nelson was saying, some of them come with very pragmatic things, like how to be healthier, more productive, how to have less sick days. Sometimes we have business people, most of the cases we have other institutions similar to ours looking for cooperation. We are good at some things, but not everything of course, so other institutions have other strong traits. But what people want the most I think nowadays, if I can put it in simple words, is a kind of a richer, deeper life. People know you are living a model life that is superficial, that is shallow, that is unsustainable. Even when you think about the economy, or whatever, it has to come from something different. There's no way for us to keep patching an old model. If the car is too old, it doesn't matter how many times you fix it, sometimes you have to throw the old model away and start with something new. That is the difficult point for human beings. Human beings don't like this deep change.

I think this is even a kind of paradox, and I bring this up in my courses many times, I say everyone discusses things about evolution, but people would like to evolve without changing. In practical terms, it's how can I be a lot more evolved, but continue to be the same kind of guy. I say that's impossible. It doesn't work like that. So how can people be attached even to problems, traumas, sometimes the identity of someone is based on traumas, the negative experiences the person had. It's so difficult for all of us to let those things go. This thing that we mentioned here in the beginning, exploration, I think is one of the best things in the human spirit, human nature, let us explore, let us see something new, let us try something different. Not all people are neophilic, not everybody likes the new. But a lot of people do, it could be a VR experience, a virtual reality experience, by the way, we are starting to use virtual reality to help people get out of the body. I forgot to tell you that. We already have a working system that simulates the person leaving the body, going into outer space and returning, but anyway, this thing of exploring is something I think that we could explore more (laugh), use more.

Nelson: I'm looking forward to using Wagner's development and combining it with some of the work that we're doing, with using vibrational patterns, inspired on the vibrational state that Wagner and Nanci have been working on, and others, for a long time, and bring in all this other technology that helps to either stimulate or monitor the mind in order to produce states of deep relaxation, of creativity and well-being. We'll be doing a lot more of that both at IAC, I-ACT is working on that, Neuma Being, the company I work at with Manori as well, a lot of cooperation, collaboration, that's the future here.

Wagner: I was going to mention that both of us had been working for such a long time together, we had different initiatives that overlapped like IAC, and I-ACT, the Institute for Applied Consciousness Technologies, and Neumascape. We are trying to get to exactly the point you're mentioning, trying to convert as much as possible of this knowledge we have, sometimes it's more academic, philosophical. Sometimes it can be mentoring sessions, it can be devices like Cymatix, helping people with that kind of vibrating pod bed, to help people to relax, to become more focused on themselves. But as we said, people cannot become dependent on the coach, the mentor. They cannot become dependent on the piece of technology. But at least these things can be a boost, can be the first kick to start movement; but people have to do their part. I don't know if I'm being pessimistic here, but it seems that people are getting lazier and lazier by the day. They want to achieve things in little time with little effort. Yes, some things can be like that but not everything. Everything that really matters in life comes with discipline, and time, and some effort. It doesn't have to be something boring or unpleasant. But time and effort, discipline, are unavoidable, and not easy to substitute. Now people want an app. Do you have an evolution app? Just press the button and you evolve. Ok, I want that.

It's interesting to study the physiological basis for laziness. Laziness is not always a bad thing. It arose because laziness was a way of saving energy. If you had little food, little calories, we would spend 1000 calories to find 900 calories to eat, so there was really a point in avoiding burning too many calories. If we didn't have anything to do, in that kind of a lower metabolism state, but nowadays I think we spend perhaps 10 calories to walk to the freezer, open the door, to get a pint of ice cream with 3000 calories. Or order delivery. So nowadays I think even the concept of laziness/productivity has to be rechecked, for instance nowadays the idea of productivity is basically of effort, of time, and even a little bit of suffering. If you don't suffer enough in your work, you're not being a good employee. Now it has to be more about creativity. How many new ideas, concepts can you come up with this year? We are about to end this year. It's a different thing.

Nelson: You come up with a model of motivation. Sometimes someone has potential, but they're just not motivated. So there's a connection between what we're talking about here, and a better understanding of motivation. Leadership a lot of times is about unleashing potential, as it should be, and the technologies and techniques we're talking about are also about unleashing potential. Because people can have a plan for their life, they can have things they can do to bring wonder, to bring joy, to help people, to bring inventions that will facilitate our life, to bring knowledge, awareness into the world. But maybe they're just not motivated at this moment. But there could be something that could unleash that motivation for them. It could be a new understanding, it could be a life experience, there could be all kinds of things that could produce a shift. Sometimes it's not a very pleasant experience that brings that shift. Probably more often than not it's an unpleasant experience. However, we don't have to wait for that to happen. I think we can go and seek out inspiration. You can find inspiration in nature, in travel, if you can have that experience within your reach. But also through things like energy work, out-of-body experiences, lucid dreams. Better role models. Better role models than you can probably find around here (laugh).

Wagner: Nelson was mentioning something that is important to us that we bring up many times in seminars, in courses, and that's this idea of life plan. It's more than just a life purpose as a general thing. We are all here to contribute to society, but we have to be more specific with it. So we have some specific mentoring sessions and courses. I was giving one course about this in Mexico City two weeks ago. One week ago it was here in Los Angeles, exactly about this. How can we work with some analytical tools to have a better idea, much closer to reality, of our life mission? What is it that we have to do in this life? We come back to that idea of being agents of evolution, but someone can be more involved with communication, or innovation, someone with politics, with restructuring of society. So we all can do something. This morning we were discussing that sometimes people see so much need in the world in so many different areas, and people feel impotent, without the means to do anything, so they don't do anything. But we have to start with the small things. If we can help one animal, one plant, one person, one family, it is already part of the whole thing. Because we have so many cognitive distortions, bias, it's amazing how the human mind is complex, it's so good at some things but has so many bugs. I don't know who developed this software. It's full of bugs.

Nelson: Bad code.

Wagner: Bad code. We have to debug our software. We have to get rid of many of these bugs. Some of them are very instinctive. Can you imagine eons and eons, hundreds of thousands of years in a particular role.

Suma: Conditioning.

Wagner: Conditioning. And being nomads in the Savannah, just walking around, gathering things. But now it has been only 10,000 years since the agricultural revolution, when we really stopped to have a more fixed community. It has been 200 years since the industrial revolution, and we're still facing the information revolution, coming faster and faster, and people have trouble adapting. How can we adapt? Our model of family, society, and friends is still pretty much the one of 10,000 years ago, with the agricultural revolution. That cannot be anymore. We are living in a different planet now, different conditions. Are we going to adapt fast enough? Let us see. As I said before, I don't think we are going to find any deeper, more permanent solution to this without thinking in a multidimensional way. Our paradigm has to be different. I think it was Einstein who said something like this, that if you keep trying and trying the same way to get different results, that's madness. It's crazy. Many times we see this in politics, in economics. We have to try different ways. We have to think out of the box.

Nelson: I think it was Fuller who said that the paradigm or framework that led to the problem, cannot be the same one that will lead to the solution. Something new has to emerge, new and better. But that's all of our collective work to figure that out. We can look to the realm of consciousness for inspiration, but inspiration is only the first 1%, the rest is perspiration, and we have to do the work altogether. If we each do a small part, we can really make a difference.

Suma: We were talking about this earlier during the break, how the subject of consciousness comes and goes in trends. Where do you see this going this time around?

Nelson: To be honest I don't know except to say that it will probably continue that way, like a wave coming and going, we just have to be attentive, take advantage of the surf when it's in our direction, and hunker down for the long term and not feel discouraged when it's not. That's really all I could say.

Wagner: The figure of speech I used during the break was of tides. We have this tide of a lot of awareness, interest in consciousness, spirituality, and energy, and then the tide goes and back again, and then it comes again. Every time it comes people say it's a new era. They discovered this or that. No, these things have been with us for centuries. We can have a little machine. Now we can have a vibrating bed, but the essence is the same as what we have already known. We know that there are so many factors converging, and sometimes they diverge, but we have to see how to take advantage of that. Some things cannot be postponed anymore. Some things we really cannot postpone anymore. Whether they're reversible or not.

Nelson: We cannot feel discouraged and succumb to apathy, and mentally check out. That's the worst thing we can do. I understand why people feel discouraged and they don't think anything can change. But that's the recipe for nothing to change. We cannot give up. We're not here to give up. Go down fighting, I don't mean physically fighting, obviously, but I mean campaigning for change, in a peaceful but not apathetic way.

Wagner: Even when we think of politics, I think there's a big distortion, bias, that is sustained by the system of trying to classify everything as being in a unidimensional line, left or right, no- there are many dimensions, can we think of someone not being left or right, but being up? Like a plane? We have to think in different ways because this conditions people to think in a very narrow way. We have to find in a different way.

Nelson: We have to find common cause so we can have coalitions and collaborations, and find solutions, instead of just classifying people and dividing them.

Wagner: This induces a lot of problems. But we know unfortunately that usually humans only prioritize something when it is the last minute. If it is studying something, if it is taking care of our health, whatever, we can postpone it until there is a crisis. I just hope we don't come to an economic crisis, a social crisis, ecological crisis.

Nelson: To me it seems we are already living in one. Hopefully we wake up in the 11th hour.

Wagner: Exactly, sometimes people need a big slap on the face, wake them up, get out of the laziness.

Suma: Is there anything else you would like to share with the viewers today?

Wagner: We covered so many things here. Perhaps I'd like to cover one more thing. Sometimes when we talk about energy, altered states of consciousness, and out-of-body experiences, some people still think in the old ways, they think this is only for gifted people, special people, they think they have to be the 'one' to be able to have it, but that is not true. I guarantee it's not so. I started having out-of-body experiences, I said, when I was young. But I have seen, met, and trained so many people who didn't have out-of-body experiences, and started having them. I wasn't born with all this sensitivity to energy, to feel this and that, the first time I got a very good friend, a healer, a medium, working with energies with me, I didn't feel anything at all, it was zero, and I could with some practice, some training, some level of discipline, with time, increase my level of sensitivity. I wrote a book about retro-cognitions because it was the kind of experience I had never had before. I thought, let me become a specialist on this so that I can create my own experience. In fact anyone can experience these kinds of things. Certainly, we have to keep in mind that people have different levels of talent. It's like if we asked ourselves, can everyone, anyone learn how to play the piano? Yes, 99.9% of people are able to learn how to play piano. But how good we are going to be is a different discussion.

Nelson: Predisposition varies.

Wagner: Exactly. So some people can develop very fast. Others will take a long time. Some people can be very technical, very mechanical. Others can be a lot more organic, inspired. So there are different styles. It's the same thing with this whole field. Anyone can learn to develop these abilities. Some people, with 2-3 weeks, start having out-of-body experiences. Some people might need 3 month, or 3 years, I don't know. But the thing is, we humans, very specific primates, we are very pragmatic. We always think, even if we don't see it consciously, in terms of cost and benefit. Cost would be how much time and effort I need to invest in this. If people don't see the benefit, sometimes it's too much cost for little benefit. But when you see you can really understand that we can make our health better, coexistence with other people, a much richer life in so many different ways, people see the benefit. I use an example, metaphorically, we ask some people, would you like to learn a different language? People say "Yes, but you know I don't have the time, it's difficult, I have a block…" And then the boss comes and says, "I'm going to double your salary to learn French, German," I can bet the person is going to learn really fast another language because now there is incentive. The person can see the benefit for that particular cost. Many times people don't really apply themselves, don't dedicate too much time to this whole field because they don't really understand the benefits of it. It's having a much, much deeper interest in life. I cannot image the reality of my life if it was just the physical things. It would be so boring, so boring, a shell, a little bit more than just what animals do.

Suma: It just feels closed off.

Wagner: Exactly. There's no perspective, like a room without a window. Yes, you survive, but what kind of life is that?

Suma: Nelson, do you want to add to that?

Nelson: I think that was perfect. But, I guess along the lines of motivation, and how it might be hard for people to try, a lot of what we're doing now is just developing techniques and technologies to get people to get a taste. A lot of what we're doing now is training more people to have these experiences, those would be the ones that are already motivated. And for those who don't quite see it yet, bring the information to where they are in their moment in life, and create some experiences where they can get a taste for what's possible. Once they get that taste, hopefully they'll be motivated to go deeper. That's really one of the things that I'm hoping to do in the future.

Suma: Thank you so much Wagner and Nelson.

Wagner: You're very welcome. It was a pleasure being here.

Suma: It was an enriching conversation. I think it has opened up a window of possibilities.

Wagner: And I would like to congratulate you for this initiative because I really think this kind of opportunity, this channel, is really important, because there are so many people still needing to have some kind of input. Even if the person is going to disagree, but at least to brew, ferment something there, so congratulations, I wish you the best with this initiative.

Nelson: I second that.

Suma: Thank you. Your experience with this subject, also the approach that you have taken of scientifically, carefully looking at these experiments is very valuable. It's a very hard road, but hopefully eventually it will pay back.

Wagner: It will.

Suma: I wish you both all the very best.

https://youtu.be/auz3bMSSNYE

10. Innovations in Consciousness Research

This interview with Nelson Abreu was conducted by Kim McCaul on the Multidimensional Evolution Podcast.

Kim: This is episode 9 with Consciousness Researcher Nelson Abreu. Welcome to the Multidimensional Evolution Podcast. I am your host Kim McCaul. If you want to find out more about life beyond the physical dimension this is the place to be. We will be having conversations to expand your consciousness, help you reconnect with your essential self, and live life as an integrated, multidimensional human being. The given subject matter is a request. Don't believe in anything including what is shared here. Experiment, have your own experiences, and always use discernment.

Nelson Abreu is a Portuguese-American electrical engineer, innovation expert, and consciousness researcher, author and educator based in Los Angeles. There he co-created the world's first Mind Spa and showroom Neuma Being. It features the Cymatix Creativity and Relaxation Recliner which we will discuss in our conversation. Nelson began experiencing and studying transformative phenomenon like the out-of-body experience in 1998. He has developed techniques and technologies to facilitate such states and presented at conferences and workshops in the Americas, Europe, Asia, and Australia. He lectures at the International Academy of

Consciousness and is a member of the International Consciousness Research Laboratories Consortium. He has contributed to several books and publications, the latest of which is Ordinary People, Extraordinary Experiences. In this conversation we talk about beneficial and limiting aspects of our cultural conditioning to applied consciousness research, the benefits of a scientific mindset, the nature of consciousness as part of the Cosmic Ecology, how technology can be used to develop greater self-awareness, and much more. Along the way, we touch on a phenomenon documented in Nelson's latest edited book, where a person claims to have received a song from the extra-physical John Lennon. Nelson kindly provided me with a copy of the song, and I include it at the end of the conversation. So if you want to hear this song performed by the man who received it, not John Lennon unfortunately, and make up your own mind if John Lennon is still writing music on the other side, stay tuned to the very end of this rich conversation.

Nelson, hey, thanks so much for coming on today.

Nelson: My pleasure. Thanks for having me.

Kim: There's so much for us to get into because we both have a shared background in working with consciousness, with the International Academy of Consciousness, which I'd love to hear from you a little bit about, but to start with, if you could tell us a bit about your own personal background, both culturally and professionally, just so people get a sense of who you are and where you're coming from personally when it comes to consciousness.

Nelson: I grew up in Portugal and my parents are from former Portuguese India. When I was growing up I didn't have many experiences that you'd consider extraordinary in terms of out-of-body experiences and things like that. I had a fairly mundane existence as far as that world is concerned, until I was around 16; by that time I had already moved to Florida in the U.S. I was in the middle of high school, secondary school, and I ran into some friends and some books about things like hypnosis, lucid dreaming, out-of-body experience; and it wasn't long before I decided that it wasn't enough to just read about it, especially given that there was this idea that you could have your own experiences and therefore reach your own conclusions. I had this Catholic upbringing which made me very open to things like the afterlife, but at the same time I discovered around that time that I had more of an engineer's mind, which meant studying the natural world, and then figuring out ways in which you can do something with that and improve the world. I was really fascinated by the idea that I could have my own experiences. I started reading about techniques that I could use and I ended up having my first out-of-body experience just using things like mantras, self-talk, self-hypnosis, and things like that. But I wasn't successful at having multiple experiences until I went to IAC, the International Academy of Consciousness. I did some training there and then I started having more experiences, especially when I learned about energy, how to control my own biofield or energy field to create certain states, like states of heightened vibration or resonance. So the vibrational state really helped me.

Kim: Nelson, there are so many strands that you just touched on that I'd like to pick up. You talked about your Catholic upbringing making you open towards the afterlife. I've also often experienced people with that background having certain reticence to approaching things in a way that aren't exactly prescribed by the church or the bible. Was there anything like that that came up for you, did you feel like you were dabbling in things that were somehow wrong initially, or was that fairly relaxed for you?

Nelson: The funny thing is that other than the fairly universal fear that everyone has of death, of the dark, of the unknown, I did experience that- I was about to have my first experience, I could feel it happening, and I then I stopped myself, I felt a vibration, I felt like I was about to take off, and I did tense up, and that was probably a result of my cultural conditioning which is being human, being afraid of the unknown, but also trepidations about am I doing the right thing, am I dabbling in something that might be evil, or am I in danger. But at the same time I'm also someone who's always been fascinated about space, about physics, science is facing the unknown, exploration; so I guess at the end my curiosity outweighed my fears. I had an inner sense that the world didn't makes sense unless there was more, and if I have the opportunity to know that there was more, it's worth the risk. What also helped me was reading about so many millions of people having experiences, and they're just fine, so inside of me I knew it was mostly an irrational fear, even though it was very real, so it helped me to take a deep breath and just ride with it, it's going to be ok, even though it doesn't feel like it's going to be ok, it will be.

Of course once I had my first experience, I got that confirmation that there's definitely nothing to fear. As far as belief structures, a lot of people are conflicted, but for me it was just a natural thing: this religious teaching was useful to me, it educated me about ethics, about having a social conscience like looking out for the little guy, and things like that that are part of the Catholic social doctrine, but at the same time I was acutely aware that the church, like any other institution, is made of humans and there's no way that they're as infallible as they claim to be, so even though I was very much part of the church, in that I did all religious rites except becoming a priest, I did first Communion, there's a second and third type of Communion you could do, I did them all, Sunday school, I was in church by my own volition every Sunday, but it was more because I enjoyed thinking about life and that was the best I had available to me at the time.

However, as soon as I discovered that I could discover things on my own, I don't mean offense to anyone, but to me personally it felt like I went to elementary school and now I could go to middle school, like another step. I never looked back; my mother didn't feel the same way. She felt I was going into the dark side, she believed she had failed as a mother, and I was going to be in eternal damnation, she didn't see it quite the same way. At one point there was an article written about a work that I presented at a conference, it was published back in Goa, in India; and my aunt came across it. I'm told that she cried because this was journalistic evidence of my damnation.

Kim: Have you been able to reconcile with your mother?

Nelson: This is what happened with my mother, sadly she suffered two bouts of cancer, and her second one was her final. As sad as that was, and as painful as it was for her especially, but also for us to see her suffer, somehow there was a silver lining there. Those situations make you take stock of life and reevaluate everything. In those final moments, where she was still able to talk to us, I made a point to be with her. I went to Portugal where she was with my sister. I wanted to make sure that I spent those moments with her while she was still sort of ok. What happened is we were watching Dr. Oz or another television show, and they had a healer who was Catholic, and who basically worked with energy to perform healing. He was essentially studying a lot of the same things I had been studying, but was using the language and filter of Catholicism. So rather than saying "I will send energy towards you" he would say something like "I will pass the Holy Spirit to you." Essentially we're talking about using energy for the purpose of healing, of therapy. She turned to me and said "Did you get the guy's name? I really need to learn more about that." I turned to her and said "Do you realize this is exactly what I've been studying, and my friends as we speak, around the world are thinking about you and sending you energy already?" She said "Wow, maybe that's why I've lived so long," because she was outliving her original diagnosis. In that moment I think she had the realization that maybe I wasn't going to hell, and maybe we're just speaking a different language, but really we're saying the same things. That was really amazing to me.

Kim: That's lovely. My grandmother was very Catholic, and towards the end of her life we had a lot of good conversations about OBEs and aspects of life, life continuing, it seemed like it was a special time to open up to a wider thinking about these topics. It sounds like for you it was really your scientific mindset that in a sense pushed you further into exploring consciousness, in a sort of experiential way.

Nelson: That's right. The desire, the need to know more, I couldn't shy away from that even if it seemed somewhat risky.

Kim: In which sense did it seem risky? In the sense that you might be doing something bad or some other aspect?

Nelson: More along the lines that I could have some undesirable outcome from doing that according to different people that talk about it. But at the same time I could see that it's a naturally occurring phenomenon, millions of people have it, it happens spontaneously, it presumable seemed to be having every night to people even if they weren't aware of it, so how bad could it really be. I knew there was a history of misunderstanding it, and manipulation to keep people from having it. Somehow my rational side was able to win the tug-of-war with my fear-based amygdala, and that turned out to be the case. Not only is there nothing to be afraid of, while it's natural to be afraid at first, the cure to most of our fears is to have this sort of experience. It's been extremely liberating to not fear death, to not fear the dark, to not be afraid of spirits, etc. etc. The only thing I fear is to live a life where I look back and feel I didn't do as much as I could to help others, to learn, I don't expect to live a perfect life as a fallible human, but I'd like to have more feelings of fulfillment than of regret. Even that, I know it won't be the end of the world if I somehow miss the mark. There's always more.

Kim: Maybe you could give us a bit of an overview of how you have come tosee life. You went from having an initial experience that you said was just like a taste, a teaser in a way, not that fulfilling, that sent you on a search to find more. Then you studied at the IAC, the International Academy of Consciousness. In doing those studies, how have you come to see life, how have you come to see human existence?

Nelson: That's a profound question. What I've come to accept is that I would like to continue to have more questions than answers because it seems like the ultimate freedom, is the freedom to ask those questions. It's almost the whole point of life to me. To have the freedom, to have the liberty to question and to pursue those answers, even though we know we may not ever reach a final conclusion, it's not as important to me to have the final conclusion, if that's even a thing. But what's really important is to have the liberty to explore those questions and the other part is not to lose sight of the fact that we are not just brains in a vat, or consciousnesses in a brain in a vat, the biggest insight I've gotten is the fact that we're not merely individuals. We are individuals but not merely that. We're really part of the planet, part of the ecology, part of the cosmos, and that everything we do has an impact on others and vice-versa. Once you realize that, not just in theory but you actually feel it, feel that you are part of the fabric of the universe and that it is in you, that you are simultaneously one but also part of the whole, that really changes you because from that point on you don't see yourself as an individual in a competitive world, you see yourself as part of a cosmic ecology where you are related. You're related to the trees, you're related to the animals, to the planet, to all cultures, to all planets, to all dimensions, the afterlife, you're just part of all of that, and you realize the importance of having genuine relationships, to really care about people, and to try and leave the world a better place wherever you go.

Of course we're not perfect, and sometimes we leave things worse than we found them, but on the whole to at least we strive for that. So one thing I sought out is how do you define consciousness, how do you define what we are. The best synthesis I've found is that we are beings that are constantly evolving, we are maturing, and we are interconnected. To me, from those insights we get a full philosophy on life, on politics, on economics, on everything, on relationships, everything can stem from those insights. The only thing I can think of that's similar is accounts that I've heard of astronauts who go into outer space, usually these are extremely intelligent and academically qualified individuals, scientists, physicists, etc. so they know all the facts that can be known about the earth and the universe, all the available best knowledge we have today, but it's different when they're up there, they feel those facts, they understand them in a visceral way, and they report feeling a cognitive expansion and a change of identity from individuals to people who are part of the planet. When they come back, they're changed forever. I think that's why when we saw those first images of the earth from outer space, it's not a coincidence that at the same time we had a huge boost in the environmental movement. We realized we are already in space. We are in a planet, flying through space. The only thing keeping us safe are things like the magnetic field of the earth, the ozone layer, and so on. And we better take care of this earth because it doesn't look very hospitable out there in the vacuum of space.

In a similar way, when I've had 1, 2, 300,000 out-of-body experiences, that's what it's done to me, to absolutely reinforce this perspective that we are part of the cosmos. The cosmos is part of us. We are part of each other. Now what I'm left with is what does that mean in practice, how does that translate into life. How should we live our lives if we're to be coherent with that insight, and that's the question I ask myself every day and in everything I do.

Kim: The account you give as being part of the ecology is really profound and important at this time because with the environmental crisis that we're having on this planet at the moment, I hear often a sentiment that humans, there is a depiction of ourselves as being false, people talk about humans as a cancer, there's this concern that there's something inherent in us that's incompatible with life on this planet when really from your account, and that's certainly my sense too, is that inherently we have the capacity to be a very important part of the planetary multidimensional ecosystem.

Nelson: And you know from your extensive background in anthropology and studying the first peoples of this world that there was a time when people, although not perfect, did live in better harmony and had more awareness of the multidimensional nature of life, so it's already shown that we're perfectly capable of doing that. However in order to break out into outer space, into technological wonders, we sacrificed a lot in terms of that wisdom. However, now hopefully, we can come back around and combine the two. We can be technologically advanced but at the same time not confuse our relative mastery of science and technology for a full account of nature, especially our own nature. And that misunderstanding can hopefully be little by little fixed. One thing's for sure, our behavior's destructive, but at the same time, we only got here because of cooperation. We could not have cities, internet, protocols and standards, roads, rules, laws and governments, and treaties if it wasn't for cooperation. We actually have done a lot of things right. We could say, it's not that we are a cancer, but we pretty much have a cancer, and the root cause of that is what's behind the behavior. Behind behavior you have our power dynamics. Behind power dynamics what do you have? You have flows of information, you have ultimately values, you have attitudes, you have also principles, but what's behind that, what's underneath all that? That's where you find consciousness, energy.

So what we can see is that if we're able to affect someone at that deeper level, then it will bubble up to changes in patterns of behavior, attitudes, values, and from there you'll see actual measurable outcomes. If we want to value for example, nature, more, than rather than having these externalities that are not accounted for in our economic systems, of course we have to assign more value to those things. Why does the GDP go up, why does the stock price go up and down, when you look deeply into it, it's not based on some kind of physical law, it's just based on value propositions and assumptions. It's really stemming from our own consciousness. The value of money is completely fictional, it's just our perception. If you change your values, you change how much you think something is worth. What we need is cultural change, cultural evolution. For me an interesting question is how do we promote this cultural change so that we place more value on the right things.

Kim: Right. One of the things as you described in your own experience, as you were connecting with the depths of your own consciousness, and you were connecting with the interconnectedness that you experience, and that intrinsically gives you a sense of the value, you start valuing yourself more, you start valuing your connection with life around you more.

Nelson: Philosophers have called that the overview effect. That's what I would like to promote more, but that's not something you can teach someone, that's something they have to experience. So how do we facilitate that experience?

Kim: Maybe we could talk a bit about that more because I know as part of your work with the IAC and maybe in other areas, that is something that you have been working with so can you talk a bit about how you facilitate that experience for people?

Nelson: I've done that through a few approaches. One, like you mentioned, over the last 20 years has been through lectures, and educational opportunities, especially with IAC, they do provide foundational training where people can learn not just theory, but most importantly techniques, where they can have these experiences and then as a result reach their own conclusions, have their own transformation. That's very important work. I still support it. I teach at IAC to this day.

On the other hand, what I've come to realize and it's something that resonates with me, is the fact that while we continue that work and organizations like IAC that do important work, there's also work that they do in terms of research; so there's really interesting research if you Google TedX and then Wagner Allegretti, you'll see some work that he's doing with detecting bioenergy using functional MRI technology, fascinating. I also interned with PEAR laboratory, Princeton Engineering Anomalies Research lab which now is defunct. Now it's called International Consciousness Research Laboratories. They did studies looking at the ability of being, the mind, or consciousness to affect the physical world, to affect machines for example, in a measurable, statistically replicable way. That's going on too. And those are ways I've tried to contribute. Education, research - but what I've found is in both of those things, I used to think that in the beginning it was just a matter educating people, showing them the evidence, and then cultural transformation would occur. You know as well as I do, that's not true. That is enough for maybe 2% of the population. Really, most people are 1) either not that interested, or 2) just outright don't want to go there, don't want to go near these subjects.

Kim: There's a gap between the information, and to create cultural change you really need to create behavioral change. People have to create their own behavioral change.

Nelson: Behind the behavior, you have the values, but how do you change the values, you need visceral experience, how do you get a visceral experience if the person doesn't want to get educated or trained. It seems like a Catch-22. That's where this third approach that I've been working on comes in. I've been working with my wife, Manori Sumanasinghe, she's an architect and has a background in marketing as well. She's originally from Sri Lanka. We are here in Los Angeles together, what we have noticed is that in our spheres, design and architecture, or engineering, I'm doing a Master's in Innovation, so I'm dealing with people in these fields: business, design, technology, what are they interested in? A few of them might be interested in taking for example, an IAC class, but most of them would find that kind of approach a little too much like taking the red pill, or jumping, like Alice, into the rabbit hole, they're not quite ready for that, or it might be off-putting, or just weird, or scary. But what they are interested in, are things that most people are interested in, for example, being happier and healthier, having more well-being, who isn't? They're interested in having less stress, less pain, less depression, less anxiety, they're interested in being creative problem-solvers, because of the professionals that they are, but most people in the world would be interested in solving problems creatively, which fits into their personal life, essentially having insight, and to just overall perform better at whatever is important for them.

What's interesting here is that I've spent so much time trying to persuade people that the out-of-body experience is more than just in your head, that it's real, that I started losing sight of the object which is that the out-of-body experience is an experience first and foremost. That's not really something you can argue with. Research shows it's largely either neutral, or actually a positive experience. People, as we said, tend to have behavioral change as a result of having these experiences, they become more altruistic, more ecological, more self-aware; that's fantastic. So suppose for a second, that we don't care so much to persuade people, right off-the-bat, about the nature of the experience, let's just think about the effects of the experience - positive behavioral change. And then it does all those things that I just mentioned that people are interested in, improve well-being, improve creativity.

Some of the best, most influential ideas have come to people in their between awake and asleep period, in dreams, in out-of-body experiences, in intuitions, amazing works of art, civilization changing inventions, like the AC Motor, mathematical formulas and solutions, so there's undeniably a whole range of benefits that these things can bring, even to people who are not necessarily looking for answers about the afterlife. With that insight, that if you approach people in a more pragmatic sense, that these are mental resources that we have, you can draw these wonderful benefits from them, then people might actually pay attention. Once people are used to having these experiences, and they don't have a stigma of being weird or anything like that, they're just mundane, normal things that we do like jogging, or yoga, which used to be considered very specific culturally and religiously, now it's just fancy kinesthetics, then guess what, people might criticize that yoga that people are doing is not the yoga that people were originally doing originally. Absolutely true. But if you go to a yoga conference and ask how many of you have had an out-of-body experience, you'd be surprised how many people will raise their hands; which means even though people don't go to yoga necessarily for spiritual insight, many of them end up getting it anyway. I think this is the strategy that we're using - meet people where they are. What are people looking for and where's the overlap in that Venn Diagram. Where is the overlap between what society is generally looking for, what we could offer, and meet them there, meet them in the middle. That's the opening point.

Kim: Where are you creating this space, Nelson? How are you creating this space to meet people where they are, where you're meeting the people who are interested in the inspiration, in the relaxation benefits, all those things?

Nelson: One way in which things just organically developed, my wife being an architect, designer, and myself being an engineer, we were working on projects that seemed desperate at the time. Manori was working on a pet quad for our ginormous cat because there was no pod that was big enough for our dear little Kitu, but at the same time she wasn't just going to make any old thing. She was going to make a beautiful pod. Over time she lost interest in the pod idea for pets, because she thought the market was already getting saturated with other designs. So she had this insight, let's make pods for people, like nap pods. She started doing that. Then she realized that I had been working on a technology that uses vibro-acoustics. That's where you convert sound into mechanical vibration. I was working with a friend of mine, Thomas Anderson that I met through ICRL, and he was working with sound and vibration already for therapeutic purposes, and what I brought to the table was, let's use the same technique but let's use it to mimic techniques that are used to create the vibrational state. That's what we did. We figured out how to use sound and vibration to guide your attention to perform this technique. In other words, instead of me teaching a class and saying "Imagine energy at the top of your head, or try to feel energy at the top of your head, and then use your will power, your attention, your intention, to drive that energy through your body, even if you don't feel it, you don't have to visualize it necessarily, but just go with it." That's really hard to do for most people. You ask them to move something they cannot feel and they cannot use their muscles, they have to use their will, it's actually very simple but also difficult at the same time for most people.

Now compare that with, "Lie down on this beautiful recliner and just allow your mind to follow the vibrations as they move throughout your body. The vibrations move from your head through the body, down to the feet, then back up to the legs, back up to your head, mimicking the techniques that we learn and teach at IAC, for example, where the energy is now moving in an oscillatory way, back and forth, slowly, and then faster, faster, until it reaches some kind of resonant peak. I was able within 20 minutes to get people with no training to have a partial out-of-body experience, not every time, but more often than I expected. That blew my mind.

Kim: Just briefly break that down a bit more Nelson. So the recliner is rigged up. Is there a sound as well, or there's just a sensation, a vibratory sensation, that travels along the length of the recliner from your head to your feet, and back up, is that how it works?

Nelson: That's right. The foundational technology is a mechanical wave that's moving from your head to your feet. And now little by little, we've been adding more features, like you can listen to different types of music, music therapy, binaural beats, or you can listen to music that was curated by different artists for that experience. But those are things that have been added since. The basic technology was that we got a massage bed and we basically rigged it up, just to see if it worked, if it was feasible. We took it to a couple of conferences, and we also had a pilot study with people off the street who don't have any background in this. It was just fun to see this be surprisingly effective, at getting people deeply relaxed which in and of itself is a huge benefit, getting to that sleep-awake state which is prime time for OBE, and then to feel energy throughout their body, occasionally people would feel like they reached some kind of vibratory state. That was really surprising.

Then what Manori has done is take that effective but rather unsightly contraption and made it into this beautiful piece of furniture. We also have an electromagnetic option that people can use that mimics some research that's been done on healing bones with particular frequencies and so on. Those are bells and whistles that we keep adding. There's more and more technology that we can layer on top of that. The key technology we're calling the Cymatix is this traveling wave that moves through your body. It's really a way to teach people to do the technique without a single word where they follow the sensation throughout their body rather than instructions on what to do.

Kim: Yeah, sounds like a great idea.

Nelson: There's a beautiful simplicity to it, but it works.

Kim: Absolutely. It transcends language barriers, or people don't have to be able to hear anything, just feel.

Nelson: Right.

Kim: Is the vibration based on a sound, because you talked about the Cymatix and you talked about translating sounds to vibrations, so is there actually an underlying frequency that you used and what is that?

Nelson: We experimented with different speeds, starting points. We tried to use harmonics of different fundamental frequencies. A lot of people are interested in, for example, tuning frequencies, if they should be based on 430 hz vs. 436. 442 hz and so on. We've followed 432 hz as a guideline because a lot of people find that meaningful. Some people find that the 440 hz that's used to tune most musical instruments is actually fundamentally disharmonious and does not benefit well-being for most people, so we figured, let's give that a try. Turns out that at least when people experienced it they responded well to it. I'm not 100% sure about the science behind it because there's not a lot of evidence behind it. It was more at an intuitive level and based on people's input. They wanted the music to be tuned to a harmonic of 432. It's just sort of panning back and forth. Thomas and I had an initial design. It worked pretty well. Then Manori and I came up with a way to improve on it, a patented system. We used it as the foundation for this technology, for this innovation we're calling the Cymatix. That's just the beginning point.

The next point will be some time next year after we get a lot of people to try the technology. To have people try it, we invested in a space here in Chinatown of Los Angeles. Manori made it very warm and welcoming, and converted a gallery into this space that we're calling the world's first Mind Spa. A Mind Spa is a new type of retail category where you can go in, it's a Mind Spa and showroom, because you go in and you're able to try different technologies that are meant to help you with your attention, your well-being, relaxation, etc. It's a little bit like a hybrid between a cafe, an art gallery, and a bit of an arcade in the sense that you have different technologies. In a gym you might benchpress and work on your legs. Here, instead of working on your body, you work on different aspects of your mind. Besides the Cymatix for example, we have the opportunity for people to try some virtual reality simulations that help induce some of these altered states. You also have headbands that are like a commercial grade EEG that measures your brain waves and guides you through meditation practice, so people are able to try different things and become more familiar with these experiences in a very practical way.

The reason most people are going to come is for getting new ideas; L.A., Los Angeles, prides itself on being the arts capital of the U.S. California is all about innovation and the arts world, Hollywood, it's a very creative town. Everyone is either inventing something, or writing a script. Sometimes you hit that creative block. What if you could go into a space and get into an altered state without having to drop any kind of substance, and naturally get to that lateral thinking, outside the box thinking, or quite literally outside the body thinking. Even though it was conceived as an out-of-body experience machine, if you will, that's not at all how we're marketing it. The Mind Spa including the Cymatix is about getting you to states that are more mindful, more creative, to help your performance. If you're a company for example, you could have this device in your company, or you could have a subscription for your employees to go to a Mind Spa. The reason you would have that is not so they have OBEs. Most companies couldn't care less. It's more because they can have more creative ideas, they can be more innovative, they can release some of their stress, they can have pain relief, and so on. We say that the Mind Spa is a way to recharge, to reconnect, and to reimagine.

Kim: It sounds like it'll be a real hub of inspiration. I get that feeling when you're talking of people dropping in, and leaving with new inspiration for whatever their creative endeavor might be.

Nelson: It's a community of people who want that. They want more well-being. They want new ideas. And generally speaking they want to apply that to make the world a better place. These are the kind of people you would want to surround yourself with anyway. But they may or may not know about out-of-body experiences, however, through exposure, through the community activities, the classes, through the technology, they will eventually probably have some of these experiences. At least many of them will. Some of them will just look at it as it was an altered state, it was really interesting, it was entertaining. Other people will see it as a tremendously insightful, creative space. Some people will have the Overview Effect and will be changed for the rest of their lives. We're open to all of it. By putting less pressure on it, by not making it about the outcome so much, by not forcing the OBE to be a thing about the Afterlife, because it doesn't have to be, it is actually a naturally occurring healthy state that everyone can have.

Kim: It's an important part of our lives right now. It's an important part of living a full human life.

Nelson: Exactly, now get to decide what you make of it, we give the people the freedom to decide what they want; but we're not so radical to say if you're not going to use this to learn about the afterlife, then none of the other benefits matter. Because, in the U.S. for example, we're facing an opioid crisis. If people just used the OBE to reduce their independence on opioids, that alone is worth it. We could save millions of lives, and that is not trivial. What do we need in the world, more money? There's so much money in this world, so many resources, so much technology. It seems what's missing sometimes is political will or insight, something that's within us, and it's just waiting to come out. If this type of technology can help people to actually do something in the world, it might actually be the thing that takes away their apathy, and that triggers their empathy, then that's worth it also. However they choose to use it, it's going to be for the best. That's our angle.

Kim: It's really great, we often see technology almost as if it's in conflict with our human nature. To see technology, the angle you're taking, and using it to enhance our nature, our depth as consciousness, our depth as beings, I think that's a beautiful fusion.

Nelson: Thank you. The hardware is still somewhat limiting because you either have to have one in your company, or a nearby spa, or shopping center, because most people are not going to have this in their home. To make up for that, and also to augment the hardware, we have already developed an app, we just have to get funding for next year to actually release it. We've developed an app, the Neuma app, that can work on its own, or it can work in conjunction with the Cymatix, and it will be a way for people to choose, for example, 'I would like to use techniques in order to become more alert' or 'actually I'm looking to relax' or 'I'm trying to get a new idea, I want to be more creative and insightful.' You can choose what you're looking for, and based on your choice, you'll be given different resources: different mindfulness techniques, out-of-body experience, energy techniques, music therapy, etc. You'll be able to run that and they'll be 5 minutes, 20 minutes, things that you can do on the go.

Kim: They can fit into your life.

Nelson: It can fit into your life. And there is one more thing which is actually, in this space called transformative technologies, Neumascape Studio and Neuma Being are pioneers in this particular field. People realize all these different benefits, it can help you have more well-being, increase your performance, help you thrive, but there's something very specific which comes into focus in my line of work, being an engineer who has primarily worked in the field, in facilities, in operations, not just in an office with drawings, is safety. If you look at industrial safety, there's thousands of injuries in every country, millions of injuries in the world every year, due to lapses of attention: distraction, rushing, fatigue. It's not training because a lot of people getting injured have been doing their job very well, flawlessly for maybe 20 years, and then they have that one day when their mind's not in the game and tragedy happens. I found a very interesting overlap here between mindfulness and safety. We are exploring that. We have a whole line of products that we're coming out with that help people become more aware, when in fact they might be getting distracted. That whole process is supported by framing mindfulness as a safety measure.

This is another way in which we can influence corporate culture by having meditation, and even things like lucid dreaming, out-of-body experience, energy training, just as resources that people can use to reduce injury and worse, just by improving mindfulness. If a lot of accidents happen because of mindlessness, then mindfulness is one of the answers. I've actually successfully spoken to management in different types of companies, in government, private, they're very receptive. I would never have imagined that I would walk into a company, teach them energy techniques, and have them be extremely receptive. It's all about the framing. "I'm going to teach you how to unblock chakras is not really going to sell." "I'm going to teach you techniques that might reduce injuries, and might reduce sick days, and by the way Aetna released a study that it could save you $2000 a year per person" and now I've got their attention. It seems like we've just had a very big marketing problem. Maybe we can reframe things and meet people where they're at. Where are they? They're at work. They're in their home. They're trying to solve basic daily problems before they can think about the nature of the universe. However, it can help them solve those "mundane" problems, which are actually not so mundane for them, and in the process they might have amazing insight, and get to where we were hoping they would get anyway.

Kim: Sounds like a really practical angle. I think once you get into the occupational health and safety space then that's really at the core that everybody in the corporate world has to be exposed to in one way or another.

Nelson: These were the last rallying words from Dr. Robert Jahn from Princeton. He was the former dean of the college of engineering. He was the founder of the PEAR laboratory. I had the fortune to have conversations with him, and towards the end of his life he told us that we studied these phenomenon in a laboratory. We obtained really objective data that was done over the course of three decades. If people don't accept that they never will. Doing more of this type of research is important, but it's not going to change everything. We've already determined that the evidence is important but not enough. Having things that we can teach people is extremely important but not enough. His suggestion was, we need people like you to show people that these things are actually useful in the way that they define useful. To you and I, there's nothing more useful than learning about the meaning of life. But for someone in their particular moment, what's really useful is - can I have the next big idea, can this thing help me reduce my pain and discomfort, and my stress. That's useful. If we can show value, then people will use it. When people use something eventually it becomes normalized, and they might even be curious to learn more. It won't be long before people are learning about energy and OBEs in schools and at work. It's just another thing that we do. More and more people will discover that yes, it does have all these everyday benefits, but maybe there's a little more to it than that.

Kim: Yes, that's really great, and I'm really happy that you get to share that perspective, that really practical perspective. We're running close on time and I would like to talk a little about your book "Ordinary People, Extraordinary Experiences." You said that Manori created a very beautiful bed, or lounge chair, and I can certainly attest to that from the photos you've shown me. It really is a beautiful piece of furniture that I feel will find its way into people's homes who can afford it no doubt, just because it looks attractive. Plus its got some amazing features.

Nelson: Thanks.

Kim: I would like at the end to talk a bit about this book "Ordinary People, Extraordinary Experiences" which I think is a great title that in itself conveys a message, right?

Nelson: Right. Dr. Torben Riise and I were at the time volunteering at IAC Miami, and we were asking questions similar to what you were asking me moments ago, which is how do we get this information out there, awareness out there, and one of the answers we came up with was to show that everyday people, who have jobs like CFO, like grocery store checkout clerks, people who are from Latin America, Europe, and people who are in their 80s, people who are 11 years old, people across demographics, that they have these extraordinary, transformative experiences, and you don't have to be some kind of gifted person to have them. We know from history that knowledge has been handed down typically through story telling, not through text books, and all our ancestors relied on that. That's why story telling is so effective to this day for cultural change. Sometimes a movie, fictional as it might be, conveys very important ideas. So we thought, let's collect stories of people we know and trust, let's interview them, let's have them write it down in their own words. Let's make a collection, an anthology, of various types of extraordinary experiences, psi phenomenon, and let's put it out there. And to make the point that this is not about self-promotion, they're all anonymous. We know exactly who these people are, but none of them are named.

Kim: I was wondering about that, why people were made anonymous.

Nelson: It was to put the focus on the experience and the fact that it could be anyone. That's the point. It's not important who they are. What's important is that we the editors know who they are and we find them to be credible. We wanted it to have variety, so there are experiences relating to telepathy, clairvoyance, energy sensations, and out-of-body experiences as well. There is even an experience of telekinesis, mediumship, and so on. That's the first part of the book, so that people can read everyday people's experiences, and be inspired by that, and raise your curiosity on the subject. Before each phenomenon there's a brief description about what they are, different ways in which we might model or explain that phenomenon, a little bit of an introduction in lay words. At the end we have more of a scholarly book end where we talk about different theories, and about out-of-body experience. Torben has an interesting discussion about the relationship between consciousness and physics, and has a couple of chapters about that. I had written chapters in other books, and there's a collection of those chapters I had written at the end of the book. They talk about science and consciousness, and different kinds of theories and hypotheses. The beginning is very practical, pragmatic, experiential, and anecdotal. The end is a more of a scholarly treatment, but still written in a way that you don't have to have a Phd to understand it.

Kim: I was curious, I noticed there wasn't any experience of retro-cognition in the book. Did that happen because it wasn't recorded in that research period?

Nelson: Exactly. It just happened that way because there were none reported in that period that we were collecting. We would have liked to include some. There were some retro-cognitive aspects in some of the accounts, like during one of the OBEs he felt like he had done it before, like he was replaying the experience, but it wasn't a retro-cognition per say, in the classical sense. We would have liked to include some, but of all the different experiences we had, there just weren't any retro-cognitions per say.

Kim: There were two experiences that I found especially intriguing and quite moving, one of them as well. It would be nice if you could finish off by outlining those.

Nelson: Sure.

Kim: The first one is the musician who ends up receiving a song from a very famous artist. Maybe you could talk about that.

Nelson: This one was interviewed by Torben. He's more familiar. It's basically a transmission via mediumship of a song. It's a type of automatic writing, but instead of being a some kind of proclamation about the nature of things in prose, it came in the form of a song. If people would like to hear the song, there's an actual composition of it. Torben would be happy to share this song. It's a fascinating idea that someone like John Lennon could pass away, but still contribute culturally, still write songs. By the same token you could think about a scientist or a writer. They're not gone and dead forever. The possibility that we might be able to reach them and then see how they see the world now that they have moved on, is a fascinating possibility.

Kim: Absolutely. And especially with the song, it really resonates with my work in Aboriginal Australia because it's a fundamental part of Aboriginal culture that a lot of songs are brought back from OBEs. So people leave the body at night, and then in the morning they come back with new songs that they've learned.

Nelson: Really, that's fascinating. I didn't know that. The only musical type things with OBEs that I've heard of is that people go outside the body, they hear angelic music or music that moves them. I've actually experienced hearing classical music, specific songs, and then I've come back and try to find out what they are. I created a little workshop where people lie down, they try to get to the period between awake and asleep. While they listen to some of this music, they might be able to connect with these other dimensions and maybe trigger something. That's fascinating, the idea that you'd go out and then return with a song, an inspired song. That's really fascinating.

Kim: It goes with the system where the authority lies with the ancestors and you can connect with the ancestors through the out-of-body state.

Nelson: That's right. Fantastic.

Kim: The other experience, I don't know if it was you who recorded it, or Torben. It's the story of, I think it's a woman, I'm not sure, sharing her father's death, and the father being a very skeptical man at first.

Nelson: Right. I collected this one. This was a CFO of a medical device company. Someone very objective, but someone who has had many experiences, and was completely open to these ideas, and very much involved in the study and education of consciousness. However, her father was very skeptical. They had an agreement that if there was life after death, whoever went first would try to give some kind of signal. For sometime she probably even forgot about that; but there was a moment in which, while she is feeling his presence and thinking about him, and thinking about that moment, a cup, a glass cup, on a wooden table, there's nothing connected to this cup, there's no earthquake going on, this is in Florida, the least tectonically active place on earth, and this cup just goes into wild motion. It's not even metallic where you might think there might be some kind of magnetic field could be in effect. It's really beyond any explanation how this cup is moving and nothing else is moving. In that moment, rather than being filled with fear, she just knew that that was the signal, that her father realized that she was right and there is life after death, and here's my sign. Even for someone that has had lots of OBEs that was really something else, to see this huge movement of a cup on a table, out of the blue, with no physical explanation of how that could have happened.

Kim: They're pretty rare those kinds of experiences, aren't they?

Nelson: They are, yeah. But they happen.

Kim: I thought it was just so beautiful and good to know that he was able to be open enough that once he moved across to the extra physical dimension that he gained his lucidity enough to come back and tell his daughter that he was still around.

Nelson: Right, fascinating.

Kim: Nelson, we are out of time now, but thank you so much for having that chat. I'm really excited about seeing what happens with your technology consciousness combination and mainstreaming all these ideas, I think it's a really exciting direction. I think you and Manori seem to be a great team combining your engineering and her aesthetics. Just quickly, the word Neuma, the name Neuma, I just wanted to clarify what that's about.

Nelson: We were looking for a name that could speak to what we were doing. After a lot of research we did come across a term from stoic philosophy, and that word was 'pneuma' with a 'P' in front of it, as in pneumatic, pneumonia, and this refers to breath, spirit, soul. So pneuma is basically the creative spirit, the soul. We see Neumascape as the sort of playground, a playscape for the creative spirit- so Neumascape. That's what it means.

Kim: Yeah, that's awesome. Beautiful. Thank you Nelson.

Nelson: Thank you so much, it has been a pleasure talking to you, and I look forward to next time.

Kim: As I flagged in the introduction, after concluding our conversation, Nelson sent me a copy of the song that one of his research participants received, and believes it was communicated to him by John Lennon. It is here performed by the man Jerry Marshall who received it. See what you think.

https://podcasts.apple.com/us/podcast/multidimensional-evolution/id1480233881

11. Neuma Being: Well-Being Technology

This interview with Manori Sumanasinghe and Nelson Abreu was featured on Mark Anielski's podcast, The Economics of Well-Being, on February 27, 2020.

Mark: Hi. I'm Mark Anielski. I'm the author of T*he Economics of Happiness*, and my new book, *An Economy of Well-Being*. Welcome to he Economy of Well-Being podcast. I believe the most important aspiration of our life is well-being and genuine happiness. But by happiness, I refer to the original Greek definition which literally means well-being of your spirit, or well-being of your soul. I also believe we have an opportunity to change the consciousness of our world and the planet by rediscovering the true meaning of the words 'business' and 'economics,' such as the word wealth literally means the conditions of well-being, from the Old English. In my Podcast I'm joined with some incredible guests and elders to talk about the development of this new economy based on well-being. I wrote about those ideas in my new book An Economy of Well-Being, Common Sense Tools for Building Genuine Wealth and Happiness. We'll explore many of those topics in these podcasts with some of my great guests. You'll learn how to adopt some of these ideas in your personal life, your business, and your community. I hope you enjoy these podcasts and feel more hopeful about the future. You can learn more about my book The Economy of Well-Being from my website economyofwellbeing.com. You can also purchase my book on Amazon as an ebook or a paper copy. Or listen to my podcasts and be inspired. Have a wonderful life.

What I'm really interested in Manori is this whole issue of well-being and architecture design and really delve into human consciousness as well, and the conditions in which human consciousness can be amplified or increased by design, basically. I've also been working with a few architects and construction businesses who are interested in this subject. It seems like early days, so we're pioneering, it would be fun to talk about what your vision is, what you're working on, introduce you to my small little audience, maybe you'll become as famous as Malcolm Gladwell, or Joe Rogan, or something like that, but probably not (laugh).

Manori: Thank you for having me here Mark. My name is Manori. I was born in Sri Lanka and I grew up there for the most part. I moved to the U.S. to study architecture in 2007 and have been here since. I went to school at SCI-Arc Southern California Institute of Architecture. It's a private avant-guard experimental architecture school. I've been interested in architecture, the building environment, design, and generally understanding what it is to be a human, 'being', the state of being in general, since I was a kid. Growing up in Sri Lanka I grew up in the middle of the war. Experiencing those kinds of traumas very early on got me set on a path to ask questions about life, like trying to understand why we are here, and what is it that we here to do. These things, my interest in design, architecture, building environment grew parallel with my interest in trying to understand what it is to be human.

Mark: How old were you when you were trying to understand being human?

Manori: I can't exactly remember to be honest, exactly when I asked these questions but I think it's around 10 or 11 because 11 was when

I started accompanying my mom to go to meditation classes. So around then, I'm a little fuzzy with the details, but I'm pretty sure it's around then, because I experienced growing up in the war, seeing people around you dead, at age 7, 8, 9 so there came this point. I was too small to understand what was going on so I put it aside, but subconsciously still tried to process the trauma and the pain. I tried to make sense of it all and then finding some comfort in the fact that I could ask these questions and possibly work towards finding some answers. That kept me going.

Mark: Wow, that's pretty intense. They say around that period of 7-9 is when we start to actually wake up and become more conscious of being human, the beginning of adulthood. It's also when your happiness is the highest, and then it starts to slide after about 12 years of age. So that's interesting.

Manori: Yeah, that's very interesting. There are enough studies to show early childhood experiences do have a profound impact. I know some of the things I experienced were quite horrific, but I don't think it got the best of me. I was able to do all these things later on, motivated by that, taking charge of that and thinking I should be able to do something. What would be the point if we are not able to do something.

Mark: So this is what drives, motivates you now, for a better world, better design, would you say?

Manori: I think subconsciously yes. Now I'm very aware of the fact that I'm one of the lucky ones. I've been very fortunate to have had the opportunities in my life, and have the support from various different people to be able to get to where I got. That gratitude is the main motivation for me to go on right now, but I think early on that was the case. Yes.

Mark: Wonderful. Wow. Amazing. So now you're a practicing architect.

Manori: I'm not a licensed architect yet. In the U.S., the process is quite long. I had my education in architecture. I practiced under some award-winning architects here in Los Angeles. I'm in the process of getting my licensure. And I went on my own last year. So I did practice architecture.

Mark: Very good. Do we want to explore anything more about your story, or switch to Nelson, then we can get into the well-being theme?

Manori: Yeah, we can switch to Nelson.

Mark: Thank you.

Nelson: I'm an electrical engineer in California. I specialize in Smart Grids, and adding more intelligence to our networks so that we can have more renewable energy, and more reliability. I'm working on a masters in Design, Business, and Technology from the University of Southern California. It's basically an innovation program. I'm having a lot of fun with that. Like Manori I've been studying consciousness, or being, since I was a child. I started around 16 when I was introduced to books and articles about lucid dreaming, hypnosis, out-of-body experiences, etc. and that awoke my interest in the matter. It didn't take long for me to practice techniques dealing with energy mindfulness and out-of-body experiences. Pretty soon I was having some wild experiences.

Mark: Did you tell your parents about it? Just kidding.

Nelson: Not really, they were pretty conservative. It took them a little bit to figure that out. I duped my sister into sending me some cash to take courses. I got really deep into it and I've never turned back since.

Because I am an engineer, in more recent years I've shifted some of my effort from teaching others how to accomplish these sorts of altered states, even though I still do some of that, now I'm collaborating with Manori to develop applications that meet people where they are in their day-to-day life, and finding the intersection between that root level of 'being' and those practices and states of mind, and everyday applications and everyday needs of society. In that intersection is where we both feel we can make the biggest difference.

Mark: That's amazing. Tell me a little bit about the technology front. People can listen to our other conversation about out-of-body, which itself is an amazing subject. Your appreciation as an engineer for the technology that's available for us to intentionally, strategically rise in our consciousness, how does that all work, what do you envision for technology and your practice?

Nelson: The first thing to mention is that the economy today, society, is already being shaped by technology in an unprecedented way. It's causing quite a bit of disruption, it's both a threat and an opportunity. It's a threat to the status quo and to our institutions, really changing the way we work, the way we live. On the other hand, it can be an opportunity. What we're seeing is things like machine learning, artificial intelligence, automation. It's doing away with a lot of jobs, a lot of tasks, that are better suited for machines and computers. On the other hand, there is the potential that it could be very liberating. Finally humans will be valued for the things that machines can't do very well, the things that make us truly human, our creativity, our empathy, both of which emerge from our being. Therefore, technologies, techniques, experiences, designs, that bring out the best of us in those terms, empathy, well-being, creativity, innovation, that will give a huge edge to any individual, any company, any society, that invests in that. There is a whole industry that's emerging, that some call consciousness technologies, transformative technologies, internal reality, there's different ways to refer to it, but essentially well-being technologies.

That is the space in which we are working, combining Manori's design expertise with my engineering background, and our common experience and passion in mindfulness and philosophy, out of the desire to enable people to bring out the best in them, so that they can go out and give their best to the world.

Manori: I think technology is one of those things, that when we watch movies and all, we think there will be one defining day when the A.I. will take over. But it's creeping in little by little already. When you call any company now you go through this automated phone system that's essentially a very basic form of an A.I., its ability to identify the things that we say and draw specific operations from that. It's around us already. One of the things that's happening with technology that I find problematic is that people in a world where we have 7.2, 7.3 billion people, I think this is a time where especially in cities, people are the most lonely than they have ever been in history. With the access to the amount of information that we have, and the technologies available, it shouldn't be the case, but it seems like the technologies have isolated us even more.

It works against us because we humans are social creatures. We went through a process or period of identifying some of these problems, and we keep seeing so many different issues popping up, and we needed to do something about it. Are we going to just passively sit there or are we going to be part of the solution? Our solution is using technology to bring people together, but establish stronger physical connections and more tangible relationships. We built a space so that people can come here, get together, and meet up, instead of being in an online forum all the time. There is an advantage doing that because you can reach somebody in Estonia, sitting here in L.A. But if you're in L.A. you should be given the opportunity to meet up with these people and establish some relationships. What we're trying to do is find a balance, do this dance between the digital and the analog.

Mark: I think you're speaking a truth, because the basis of happiness is relationships. It's the primary determinant according to psychologists. It's interesting that we're in this world of A.I. and yet I jokingly say what happened to original intelligence, or the original capacity of human beings for consciousness, as some would say, these many gifts of the spirit that we have. If anything we've lost the ability to practice them in relationships. Sounds like you're creating the space for us to renew that deeper wisdom of our human journey which is that we are relational creatures.

Manori: Yeah, absolutely. I'm constantly fascinating by humans, and animals, and even plants. They're the greatest machines that we know right now. We create amazing rockets, and all the things we're able to do, but it comes nowhere close to what a plant is able to do when a human breathes.

Mark: Yes, exactly. I'm a forester, and we're still amazed at how photosynthesis works. It's true. When I watch Jack Ma and Elon Musk have a conversation about artificial intelligence I thought it was fascinating for these two guys to talk and I think Jack Ma was making the point that we're still beings of relationship. He said, why do you want a one way ticket to Mars when we have a lot of stuff here yet to do here, to renew the relationships that maybe have been damaged. We can't blame technology on all of it.

Nelson: We are definitely seeing that people are suffering from loneliness, urban fatigue, pain, actual physical pain, and so on. But on the other hand, we are seeing a growing interest in things like mindfulness meditation. There's more and more research coming out that these types of practices can help reduce anxiety, stress, depression, pain levels, and also can be a source of vitality, energy, as well as occasionally people in these states experience cognitive shifts, cognitive expansion, where they feel one with the universe, one with nature, might feel closer to others, might have a renewed sense of purpose. In other words we have so much money in this world, so many resources, and it seems like what's sometimes missing in order to solve our global crises, is within us already. But we have to unleash it, the creativity, the innovation, but basically the new way of seeing the world that's more empathic, more ecological, and that's what we hope to bring out with technology and design. Technology is pretty straightforward for example, we know that these techniques have results, mindfulness techniques, altered states, so the purpose of the technologies are just to get you there more frequently, more often, more effectively. It's fairly straightforward.

So for example, the Cymatix is a technology that we created that includes vibro-acoustics, meaning sound into vibration, and we just use that vibration to create a traveling wave, that moves from the top of your head throughout your body, down to your feet, and then back up. So your mind follows this vibration, so where the vibration goes, your attention goes, and before you know it, you're actually doing a technique, a mindfulness technique, that consists of moving your attention from your feet to your head and back. In other words, you're using technology to guide people to do a mindfulness technique, and then you get them to that state. There are other technologies out there that use pulses of light, for example, to help stimulate the body and get it more prone to an altered state. We're developing an app that goes along with that, that guides you to reach those states more frequently. The technology portion is I think very straightforward, it's just a matter of R&D. From my point of view, something that's pretty interesting is the role of design for well-being and that's what Manori is bringing in to this conversation. I like when she talks about the power of design to bring dignity, to stimulate the thing that makes us human, the design component of technology.

Manori: I think it needs to be broken down differently. The way we approach everything in life right now is super specialized. We need to look at things in a more holistic, not in the sense of spiritually holistic, but I'm thinking about what's our place in the world, how we respond to all these changes that are taking place. The way I look at all of this is technology, our bodies, the environments that we are in, the stuff that we're interacting with, all these are interconnected, so we need to look at it like how do we integrate some of these aspects, as many components as we are thinking about finding solutions. I think that was the arrival point of me coming up with this ecosystem, Neuma Being. There's the human body that has specific requirements, and the mind that has specific needs, and then the daily life, the external factors that we have to deal with, and the available technologies, and then the component of community and relationships. I looked at all of it. I will talk about the design of Cymatix in a bit. But I think in order to understand what it is we're doing, we need to look at the overall picture first, then break down the individual components that way it makes sense.

Over the past few years, being in Los Angeles, working in architecture, I was experiencing a lot of stress, commuting, and navigating day to day life. I know I'm not the only one who was going through it. I saw it enough. The world is very demanding right now. It can take a toll. I was looking for resources to help with that. I knew there were the tools of meditation and mindfulness, that was there, but then what about being able to exercise some of those at a workplace. When you're working 12, 14 hour workdays sometimes to meet a deadline, I wished there was a space, and some moments when I could use some of those techniques, so that I could recharge, and not get so carried away with all the tasks that we had to do. I was looking around and there was really no one place where you can find all these resources. There was a meditation app, and then if I wanted to talk to people who had a similar interest, I had to go to a different thing, and different technologies for different parts of it. There was really a gap. We know stress is one of the biggest problems in the 21st century, people being overworked and burnt out, despite the fact that we have amazing technological advances, people are working more nowadays. That impact that problem has on people is going to be felt in many parts of our society, economically, financially, but also the well-being overall as a society. We're beginning to see some of the effects of this disintegration that's happening.

I was thinking there must be something we should be able to do. Having the knowledge that we have, and the tools that we have, at least for some people, the things that we create should be able to help. Out of that need came about Neuma Being. There has been several projects that Nelson and I have been working on, on the side. He has been working on this technology for using sound waves to mimic this mindfulness technique that he just explained a little while ago. I had come up with this piece of soft furniture that's helping people with relaxation. This is furniture that's able to create this personal space for people to recharge. He's been working on an idea for an app, and I've been working on an idea for an app. For years we've been talking about bringing together people who have similar interests, and similar challenges so that we can work together and grow together.

One day in 2016 I think, there was this aha moment, maybe we should smash them all together in one ecosystem. I'm really bringing in a lot of the aspects of my interest in design, and mindfulness, and even technology. The school that we went to really was experimental in the sense that we were looking at how to do architecture and design with robotics and with algorithms, and new kinds of material, bringing some of that knowledge into this project. We managed to create this beautiful piece of furniture that we prototyped and launched on November 15th. It's called the Cymatix. It brings together ergonomics, mindfulness technology, design, all of these things. It's really a personal space for somebody to take a quick recharge, reconnect with themselves. And then with that came this idea maybe we should have a space where we can demonstrate what we are doing and what we are talking about. We ended up taking this beautiful art gallery in Chinatown, Los Angeles, created this space called Neuma Mind Spa and Showroom. Right now we have that piece of furniture and a showroom condition where we are going to start increasing our library, adding to our library of other tech, in this field, and showcase all the things so that people in somewhere like Los Angeles, or any other big city, or anywhere really, if they're experiencing high stress, or they're having a hard time relaxing, and they don't have the time to drive to nature, they can just stop by for 20 minutes and recharge, reconnect, and use that as a springboard for reimagining what it is that they have to do next.

Mark: That's impressive. So the space is both for individual recharge on your newly designed furniture but also space for a collective gathering; what is the collective gathering?

Manori: Because of the nature of the space, we actually have space to gather 20-30 people at a time, just bring together people and do different types of events where we can give the platform for people to establish connections and figure out what emerges. Over the last one and a half years I felt this appreciation for the emergence of things, when you give it a little feel and see where it goes. I'm really curious to see what could happen in this space. I've already reached out to different groups of people over the past four weeks. I think we had nearly 175 people coming here to plug into this group.

Nelson: It's a diverse group of people. We've had Rabbis, we've had engineers, architects, statisticians, artists, government officials.

Mark: Have you had economists yet? Just kidding.

Nelson: Maybe one or two. These are people who are obviously interested in the intersection of well-being, design, technology. What happens when you bring these people together? That's part of the fun, is the idea that you create an environment that's creative, has technology to be creative, and then collaboration just occurs, and then you see what emerges, new technologies, new initiatives, all within this focus of improving well-being of individuals, companies, and communities.

Manori: I think one of the things that I find really interesting is that over the past few years, people are becoming more and more polarized. So I see our space as a place where they find commonalities instead of polarization. Figuring out how to work together and hang on to the things that we share in common rather than focusing on what make us different.

Mark: I don't want to go down this rabbit hole, but I want to ask a couple of questions. Nelson, you were born in Portugal. You have Indian roots. Manori, you're from Sri Lanka. Your observation as a newcomer to America, I'm Canadian and I in part, I think part of the issue that I see has its roots in our economic thought which is individualism, materialism, consumption, a kind of hedonism that's taken hold and become more amplified in the last 30-40 years and it seems that this is part of the scourge. If happiness is mostly about relationship, 40% they say is about relationships, is the key driver of happiness, then what you're doing is helping to reestablish those pathways of relationships that we have lost, and there's a hunger for in our very divided, and it's partly part of America's brand too, so what do you see among the younger people, is there an emerging, is there an awakening happening that's going counter to the individualism that we've seen so rampant.

Nelson: When I moved from Portugal to the U.S., I definitely felt a culture shock right away, that people didn't have time to have tea with you. Everybody seemed to be going in fast forward motion, and that meant people didn't have time for reflection, for simple relationships, that was a bit of a shock. On the other hand, the idea that people are not up your business all the time and you can be so independent is also refreshing. I noticed that neither the Asian community tendency nor the American individual tendencies had all the answers. They both have pathologies and also at the same time they have this refreshing aspect to them. Our task and opportunity to travel the world and see how people do things differently, find that we are all human, and then take the best of each one, or try to emerge something that combines the best of all of them. For example, capitalism has a lot of negative side effects, like you mentioned, overconsumption and so on, the environmental impacts of all of that, the social and psychological impacts. On the other hand, have you known in the history of the world any system that has brought out also the best in people as much. When you bring people together, as long as they have a sense of purpose, which is the other big part of happiness, a group with a shared sense of purpose, they're excited, they're solving real world problems, they're prototyping and creating, bringing out the best in each other, and collaborating because people come from different backgrounds in technical design, business, and anthropology, you put all these people together and they make amazing things that improve everyone's life. You see the potential come out. While it's not perfect, it also has this ability, entrepreneurship, and collaboration can also be magical somehow. Maybe our role is to figure out how to reimagine everything.

Taking the best of what we know and bringing some new things from within our creative depths. This is what excites us the most. We don't know the answers. But we know that we do need to improve economic systems, work places, work, because people are not well at work many times, also how we go through life could improve. We're not here to prescribe the answers to others, but we are here to say that it is possible to create environments, to use technologies and techniques that will help people get those insights, those breakthrough moments. In a way we see this space, Neuma Being, as a generator of breakthrough moments.

Mark: That's fantastic. I know in my own experience I've been involved with circle dialogue, or processes, in which you realize that, I always say that a lot of the answers to our questions are found in the circle if we open up the conversation to our lived experience. That itself is very powerful because we may feel that we're alone in our experience but in fact there's someone in the room that has something to share, that we can learn from. And that's very indigenous, I work a lot with first nations and they understand that the idea of the sacred circle, or the hoop, is really critical. I think what you're touching on is the need for balance, diversity is strength actually, not monocultures, but what can we learn from different cultures or different approaches, it could be spirituality, and these different modalities, so that's what's exciting to me about the future, the path ahead, that's also my intrigue, this idea, can well-being be in a sense baked into design. One of the things I want to touch on Manori and Nelson too is, with this notion of frequency, I'm sure you studied the 7 chakras and they have different frequency profiles, in fact some say every creature, everything in the universe has a unique frequency address. The human body of course is a sequence of progression frequencies, do you in your technologies aspire to helping to restore the vitality of your chakras, the frequencies, in which harmony can be found again or rewired in the body?

Nelson: I'm an electrical engineer. I study and use things like electromagnetic fields. I have a very technical definition of frequency and so on. But I understand this is more of a metaphorical use of those terms. In a metaphorical sense we could probably go down that alley. But what we're trying to do also is, even though I've studied a lot of literature and different philosophies, we're trying to approach it in a very pragmatic sense. The idea is yes, we want to bring out more vitality in people, more creativity, and a big part of that, some people would interpret as unblocking our human energy field and making it more intensified.

Mark: Or at the very least being cognizant that we come in because we experience a blockage of some kind. We don't necessarily know where it is. I'm going a little bit in the woo woo here, if your base chakra is blocked…

Nelson: Institutes of health (NIH) in the U.S. study this, and they study mostly as a model to talk about it. But here's a beautiful thing. The reason we've been able to attract such a diverse group of people to Neuma Being is that we don't start with the theory and the models and the language but we go directly to the experience. And we found that pretty effective.

Manori: I think whether people use different terminologies or how they choose to describe all of these things, I think everyone can relate to feeling good or feeling bad.

Mark: Exactly, very simple language. Or experiencing well-being or not.

Nelson: A creative block or not.

Manori: Exactly. Everybody can understand the output. Everybody can understand what they're feeling. Whether the mechanics behind it has to do with vibrations or frequencies or energy. I think regardless of that, we all sort of know what the outcome is. What we're trying to do is, trying to talk about this in a way that anybody can relate to. I'm not interested honestly in having people buy my philosophy of how I approach life. I'm more interested in people using these tools to improve their life. This is circling back to the question that you asked before. We are individual beings with individual needs. But being individual essentially means that you are able to be yourself and do what's right for you while being in a path. The tools that we're creating and the techniques that we are putting out then, and the way that we're approaching this whole thing is I'm not trying to get you to be what I am.

Mark: Right, this isn't religion or faith.

Nelson: It's more about experiencing an improvement and a shift.

Manori: That's the same philosophy I look at with architecture. One of my heroes said architecture essentially has to do with well-being. There's no question about it. We don't talk about it explicitly. I think designers understand this but they don't talk about it much. But for me that part of the conversation is so important because we live in built environments. Unless you go on a hike and go to the wilderness you're in built environments all the time, be it roads, be it buildings, things that you interact with, these are all built environments. If we build it keeping the well-being in mind and not treat humans as parts of a machine, like a cog in a machine, then perhaps we would cater to well-being better than trying to think about productivity or just about efficiency. If humans were easy to understand, I don't know what we would be doing. Humans are very complex.

Mark: We would be more automated. Even well-being could be automated I suppose. But we're not. We're complex.

Manori: We're complex. We don't act the most rational way. We cannot explain why we like something sometimes. Throughout history, art and architecture have tried to define the reason, like if you look at classical architecture they were saying what's most desirable is to have symmetry and proportion, and during the modernist era, or the post-modernist era, that was challenged and asymmetry was favored. These thoughts are shifting and we really don't fully understand what it is to be human. I find it also quite beautiful because we're in this together, we're in this mess together. We do beautiful things despite everything once in a while going wrong. I think it provides amazing opportunities for us to actually look forward, be able to think and dream and imagine.

Mark: I think that's where we find common thread here in my work as an economist. As I wrote about, the word wealth means the conditions of well-being and the word happiness in Greek means well-being of your spirit or your soul. It's interesting that we could reverse it and say being well. It's so encouraging to hear you in this field of design and architecture saying of course, it should be about well-being. It's nice to hear that these words are really common in our disciplines, but have maybe been forgotten.

Nelson: Going back to the Cymatix which is part of the Neuma Mind Spa, one of the first things that people have told us, before they even tried the underlying tech, is they're immediately struck by for example, how welcoming the environment is. They look at the spa and say it's beautiful. You get the idea that people are responding to the fact that a designer, a human being has consciously, deliberately put something out with the explicit intent of honoring that which makes every one of us human. The idea that you can experience something at that level, beauty, or surprise, the light, those are the things that make us human. As a non-designer, one of the things I've learned is really to appreciate what a designer and what an architect brings in. Because my first prototype worked, but it was ugly. It wasn't easy on the eye. An engineer might think who cares, it works. But now when you look at it you say, that is not just a thing that has to work, it's not just a technical thing, because we are not just zeros and ones, we have this inner rich life. When you take that into account people notice and people appreciate it. It is a sort of richness as well.

Mark: I have another question for Manori on actually the point Nelson you just made. This burning question I've had for designers, and I'll reference, you probably know the name Ilse Crawford in London, I saw her and her husband were on a Netflix program about design. They said 'well-being,' I said what, so I paused it and I had to write it in my book, because I thought that's unbelievable, she uses that word. I think her team is mostly women. They design for Ikea which is apparently very challenging because you have to design with lots of cultures and people in mind. But when you're thinking about design are you kind of stumbling around to find a design that might be appealing, beautiful to you in your sense of beauty, or are you tapped into what might be more universally considered beautiful or make you feel a certain way.

Manori: It's a very good question and it's a hard question because beauty I think is very subjective based on the things that we've experienced and based on what we've been exposed to really, and what you grew up with, and everything. Everyone knows that beauty is in the eye of the beholder. I think there's a certain depth to that in that sense that only you know how it is to experience your life through your eyes, not even your siblings, not even your twin. So to be able to design something that universally works for someone, and they find it beautiful, I think is that elusive thing that one could chase because what would that be? For me it's not feasible to design something that works for everyone in terms of aesthetics. However, designers always pay attention to other factors. A good design is not essentially just beautiful, but it needs to work, there's a utility in beauty in the sense that, is it creating delight? That is subjective, but you try to do it as democratically as possible meaning you try to make it accessible to as many people as possible. I know one of the approaches to design is that you either go for it and try to find the lowest common denominator, or you go the opposite. Example: the Tesla Cybertruck. People are very polarized about what they think. Some people love it, and some people absolutely hate it.

Nelson: A few people are neutral.

Manori: Few people are neutral. It's the intention of the designer also, you cannot ignore the intention of the designer, the designer was trying intentionally to create this truck.

Nelson: It also looks that way for a reason. If you look into it, the manufacturing is completely different, which allows it to be much more affordable, etc. etc. So it's not 100% arbitrary either.

Manori: There's a certain efficiency.

Mark: There's a utility kind of attribute to it too.

Nelson: It almost looks like an air foil so there's a lot to it, engineering and design came together.

Manori: The concept that the designer is working with, as a designer I find it really fascinating and I appreciate that a lot, but I know a lot of people may or may not be aware of that, but I always find it interesting, something that seemingly, a very simple decision, or a very simplistic design, actually had a lot of thought behind it. You see that often. The things that seem simple, the most minimalistic, are the most difficult ones to execute.

Nelson: You said something, you were quoting a designer, something about the best design is invisible.

Manori: Yes. Buildings essentially, that's what I find the most beautiful about buildings, is that, we designers and building professionals, we spend a good few years coming up with that, conjuring that, and then once it goes into use, people usually adopt it to whatever way they choose to use it. We cannot control how people are going to use it. But it's in the background. It's like a blank canvas. Even if you go to a museum. Outside may be stunning, but usually on the inside, the art needs to be the center stage, not the building. And that's how it is with a lot of buildings that you go to. The building's just there, silently, just watching over everyone, giving and making the space for people to grow, to do whatever it is that they need to do, to have conversations or to study or to sleep, or to have connections, interactions, it's all happening within that space, but it's there. It's this member of any activity that's there (invisibly), which I find really fascinating. I think a lot of good designs are like that no matter what scale, be it a pencil or a building. It's just performing a task, but invisibly present at all times.

Nelson: What I keep thinking about when you speak about design, the more I learn about it is empathy, because when you design something you have the people who are going to use it in mind, and you're trying to understand their needs, and you're actually talking to them. To build what we built, we talked with so many people, we've gotten their feedback, it's not done in a vacuum. You're always thinking about that person, their well-being, their internal response, I think that's fascinating as well.

Mark: It's very fascinating. Wow. This has been a superb conversation.

Manori: Thank you for having us. We really enjoyed being here.

Mark: Thank you. I'm cognizant of time, including my time because it's one hour later here. But I'd like to close off with any further reflections. You're located in Los Angeles Chinatown. So you do acupuncture, no I'm just kidding. Are you officially open, how does one find you? You can go to our website NeumaBeing.com. You can come and visit us. You can make an appointment and come and use the technology that we have there. On the website there's a place where you can book an appointment to experience some of the technologies, but you can also, if you're unable to do that, or you don't want to do that, but you just want to find out what we're doing, you're most welcome to just come by, drop by, and I'm here.

Mark: Fantastic. Do you have plans to commercialize?

Manori: We are going to check and see how it will be received by the community for a few months. If all goes well, yes we will commercialize because we do see a lot of potential in the Cymatix and the Mind Spa.

Nelson: People have been inquiring from different industries: well-being, medical, spa/hotel, spaces, airports, anywhere that needs to add well-being, like creativity, there we are. I'd like to make a reflection that the future of our economy, of society, is definitely shaped by both creativity and empathy. If you look at the reports on what are the skills that future companies are looking for, number one is soft skills, creativity is a big part of it, and critical thinking. Essentially these types of experiences that we are providing can give an edge to any person or company. There's no coincidence that we are here in Los Angeles. Los Angeles is considered the creative capital of the U.S. We have Hollywood, we have a lot of other industries, a lot of start-ups as well, a lot of artists. This is a creativity hub as well, a manufacture of new ideas. So we welcome anyone who wants to try to get that new idea or just get new experience, enjoy new experience, or feel better by using techniques and technologies that we've been developing. We'd love to meet them.

Manori: Or simply just come and try the fun things that we're creating. We want all of these to be fun also because it's not about suffering. I think there's enough suffering.

Mark: I love those closing reflections, empathy, and just simply feeling better, that's probably as simple as you can get, as compelling a plug. Thank you so much to both of you.

Manori and Nelson: Thank you. Thanks for the opportunity.

The Tao of the Dow

12. Where Do Great Ideas Come From?

Innovations, big and small, often come from turning an everyday problem or gap into an opportunity. However, sometimes they seem to come out of "nowhere": in dreams, in nature, while sipping tea... 72% of people report creative ideas in the shower: "the relaxing, solitary, and non-judgmental shower environment may afford creative thinking by allowing the mind to wander freely, and causing people to be more open to their inner stream of consciousness and daydreams."

At Neuma Mind Spa, in Los Angeles, individuals and teams can have similar results employing time-tested techniques and cutting-edge transformative technologies like the Cymatix. By tapping into different mental states, they improve the odds of that magical moment of lateral thinking, awe, inspiration or creative insight.

Ideas for some of the most interesting works of art, design, science and engineering have emerged in lucid dreams and hypnogogia (the period between wakefulness and sleep) and other altered states. In fact, the concept for our own Cymatix came to Neumascape Studio creative director Manori while she was in bed falling asleep. Some famous examples of reported creations include:

The Sewing Machine
Google
The idea for the movie The Terminator
The idea for the movie Inception
H.P. Lovecraft's Necronomicon
Tintin In Tibet

The Tao of the Dow

Dr. Jekyll And Mr. Hyde
Stephen King's Misery
Srinivasa Ramanujan's theta math functions
Frankenstein
Yesterday by the Beatles
Einstein's Special Theory of Relativity
Benzene
The shape of DNA
The periodic table of elements
Descartes' insights into the scientific method

Of course, there are usually real, domain knowledge and experience (sweat and tears) that are accumulated before that magical moment. Small group brainstorming and conversations can play a huge role too — though they can also represent noise that overwhelms your own muse. It is a balancing, blending act.

Many already recognize innovation as an alternating process between solo and group dynamics, focused and diffuse states of mind, convergent and divergent thinking, centripetal and centrifugal processes. Transformative technologies and mindfulness and altered states techniques can give you an edge.

Mind Spas: The Wave of the Future

A gym, a launchpad, a spa for your mind…came to Chinatown in the Fall of 2019 courtesy of Neuma Being, a project by Neumascape Studio and the brainchild of Manori Sumanasinghe, an SCI-Arc graduate and Sri Lanka native. Los Angeles residents and visitors are able to experience Neuma Being's Neuma Mind Spa & Showroom and its highlight feature, the Cymatix Lounge. This curated creative space has a relaxing and welcoming ambiance that puts visitors at ease. With ample natural light, tall ceilings, and a pop of color and texture, lounge furniture, along with many plants creates a unique vibe that is a hybrid between a spa, café, and an art gallery.

Where Do Great Ideas Come From?

Neuma Being's goal is to become a new kind of millionaire organization: one that directly or indirectly touches the lives of a million people with its creations. Its designs are meant to help urbanites recharge, reconnect, and reimagine to improve well-being and performance. The spaces, technology, and experiences it provides help recharge their energy, reconnect and promote empathy, and reimagine things by igniting creative expression and problem solving.

By booking a session at the Neuma Mind Spa, guests can receive a unique experience with a warm welcome. A typical session includes a personal evaluation, exclusive guided session in the Cymatix Lounge, feedback, and some pampering. The showroom features demo units of other transformative technologies that are geared towards optimizing human well-being and performance. Additionally, Neuma Mind Spa hosts in-person and online monthly activities aimed at promoting a sense of community around well-being, creativity and leadership (Neuma Community).

The Cymatix Lounge is a unique hand-crafted piece of designer furniture with embedded technology. The organic design of the Cymatix pays homage to the womb of a mother – the most primal safe space to grow, to heal, and to nurture. It is a semi-enclosed space that gives privacy to the user without claustrophobia. The Eames Chaise Lounge by Charles and Ray Eames influences the seat of the Cymatix. Seat ergonomics account for various body types, while the gel memory foam cushion and the supple perforated faux-leather provides for optimal comfort. All of the technology is embedded underneath the seat.

Patent-pending vibro-acoustic technology and electromagnetic tech make the Cymatix much more than a beautiful piece of furniture. A pilot study demonstrated that this transformative technology that subconsciously mimics energy mindfulness techniques, is highly effective in producing quick and deep relaxation. Users typically describe feeling like they are in a type of relaxed, lucid sleep, floating and experiencing pleasant sensations throughout the body.

This rapid and profound relaxation helps users achieve healthy states of awareness and mindfulness associated with reduced pain, stress, and depression; enhanced overall well-being, insight or creative problem-solving; and improvement in decision-making. Some users have been able to attain profound insights that trigger a more universal sense of purpose and connection with all of nature and human-kind - the kind of transformation that fuels visionary leaders. It can be compared to the "overview effect" experienced by astronauts in outer space, near-death experiencers, some users of floatation tanks and advanced yoga and meditation practitioners. Finally, Neuma Being has designed the Neuma App to support the Neuma Community and to augment the Cymatix Lounge experience. The app features one-of-a-kind, easy-to-follow, guided mindfulness and altered states modules based on decades of personal practice, teaching, and R&D by the founding team. The complete system will be available for distribution for leisure and entertainment, therapeutic, professional and athletic performance, and creative environments.

Neuma Mind Spa, the Cymatix Lounge, Neuma Community, and Neuma App: together, they comprise the Neuma Being ecosystem. Neuma Being plans, this way, to help Angelinos achieve optimal states of body, mind, and spirit aka "our best selves." Looking at the state of affairs in this world, and the needs of the new economy, we cannot seem to have enough motivation, empathy and problem-solving mojo. Los Angeles, an international capital for the creative arts, and no stranger to mindfulness, well-being, and pop up experiences, seems like a fitting home. Contact hello@neumascape.com to receive ongoing updates. The Neuma Mind Spa & Showroom is located at Neumascape Studio on 443 Jung Jing Road at the picturesque Chinatown Central Plaza.

Need an assist to improve your focus and energy? Looking, instead, for a creative breakthrough with some out of the box thinking? Either way, Neuma Being can help through techniques and technologies curated for your creative, high-performance mind. Book your Neuma Mind Spa experience today!

Hypnogogia: Something Curious Happens Before You Fall Asleep

Emmanuel Swedenborg and William James, among others, observed that there is a brief time, between waking and sleep, when reality begins to warp: hypnagogia. Rigid conscious thought starts to give way into the early-

Where Do Great Ideas Come From?

stage nodding off in this hypnagogic period. With one foot in wakefulness and one in dreamland, we oscillate in and out of vivid images and sounds that begin to lap into your mind. Our thoughts become a little more lose, but we may be able to remain merely amused observers.

L.A.'s Neuma Mind Spa has designed experiences for individuals, couples and teams to give rise to the kind of diffuse state of mind that can finally allow all those hours of focused learning, thinking, and doing to translate into creative insight. Your breakthrough solution or your next project may already be incubating in your subconscious.

Aristotle was an early fan of the power of hypnagogic napping and lucid dreaming, where you become aware that you dreaming: "For often, when one is asleep, there is something in consciousness which declares that what then presents itself is but a dream." A well-known fan of creative naps, Thomas Edison used a hypnagogic technique. Holding a handful of steel ball bearings, as soon as his hand relaxed, the bearings would fall into a bowl and wake him so he could jot down his thoughts.

Salvador Dali, whose art often carried dreamlike quality, would reportedly rest in a chair, holding a large key between his thumb and forefinger above a plate on floor. Eventually, he would drop the key onto the plate and the noise would snap him back to waking consciousness. Einstein would also micro-nap sitting on an armchair, holding a pencil or spoon and begin to doze off for similar effect.

JFK's workdays were 12 hours long, but he relied heavily on naps to keep him alert. He learned the technique from his predecessor, Dwight Eisenhower, who, in turn, took his cue from Churchill. Churchill understood how much a 20-minute period of calm can do for one's productivity and creativity. "Nature has not intended mankind to work from eight in the morning until midnight without that refreshment of blessed oblivion which, even if it only lasts twenty minutes, is sufficient to renew all the vital forces... Don't think you will be doing less work because you sleep during the day. That's a foolish notion held by people who have no imaginations. You will be able to accomplish more. You get two days in one — well, at least one and a half," he said in his book The Gathering Storm.

Book your Neuma Mind Spa experience today and see what our techniques and technology can do for your creativity, vitality, and overall well-

The Tao of the Dow

being. Don't have a ton of time? Remember Churchill's advice about accomplishing more by taking a few minutes for yourself and note that we have 20-minute and 50-minute options available!

13. Consciousness Hacking the Nervous System

Mind Your Inflammation!

Training in meditation and other mindfulness-based techniques brings lasting improvements in mental health and quality of life for patients with inflammatory bowel diseases (IBD), according to a study in the journal Inflammatory Bowel Diseases. Anxiety, depression, and decreased quality of life are common in patients with IBD. The Mindfulness-Based Stress Reduction (MBSR) intervention consisted of eight weekly group sessions plus a daylong intensive session, led by an experienced instructor. The program included guided meditations, exercises designed to enhance mindfulness in daily life, and group discussions of challenges and experiences.

Sixty (60) participants were also encouraged to perform daily "mindfulness meditation" at home. Thirty-three (33) patients agreed to participate in the MBSR intervention, 27 of whom completed the program. Ratings of mental health, quality of life, and mindfulness were compared to those of the remaining 27 patients who chose not to participate (mainly because of travel time). The MBSR participants had greater reductions in anxiety and depression scores, as well as improvement in physical and psychological quality of life. They also had higher scores on a questionnaire measuring various aspects of mindfulness--for example, awareness of inner and outer experiences.

What about the inflammation itself? A 2013 study pointed to a possible explanation for evidence that suggest chronic stress leads to excessive inflammation in the body, which in turn, is thought to be a key driver of heart disease, diabetes, and other chronic conditions. Researchers found that chronic stress changes gene activity of immune cells before they enter the bloodstream so that they're ready to fight infection or trauma -- even when there is no infection or trauma to fight. This then leads to increased inflammation. A study published in the February 2014 issue of the journal Psychoneuroendocrinology shows that mindfulness can limit the "expression" of genes associated with inflammation.

Reducing stress, as a result, becomes of major importance to prevent disease and ease its symptoms. We can look to consciousness-related practices as part of stress-management, along with sufficient sleep, diet, exercise, strong social relationships and other healthy practices. Studies show mindfulness appears to reduce blood pressure, pain response, stress hormone levels and even improve cellular and neurological health.

While you can't control the automatic stress response, you can promote your own relaxation. Slow, diaphragmatic breathing, activates the vagus nerve, which the brain uses to communicate with the entire body. Even one conscious breath begins to activate your vagus nerve: your heart rate slows, your blood pressure drops and your body enters a state of mental and physical calm. A similar state is experienced when one practices chi exercises. Your heart rate slows, your blood pressure drops and your body improves its state of mental and physical tranquility.

It is thought that the inflammation response triggers an increase in inflammatory molecules (cytokines) that can block key hormones and neurotransmitters - such as serotonin and dopamine - that affect moods, appetite, sleep and memory. On the other hand, positive emotions, like the experience of awe, could potentially help counter inflammation. Such positive emotions are associated with positive relationships, exposure to beauty (in nature or in the arts), the joy of discovery which begins with curiosity, and expansions of consciousness studied and promoted by Neuma Being, could potentially help counter inflammation.

What happens in Vagus

The vagus nerve starts in the brainstem, just behind the ears. It travels down each side of the neck, across the chest and down through the abdomen. 'Vagus' is Latin for 'wandering' likely because its nerve fibres wander throughout the body, networking the brain with the stomach and digestive tract, the lungs, heart, spleen, intestines, liver and kidneys, not to mention a range of other nerves. It is made of thousands and thousands of fibres and 80 per cent of them are sensory, meaning that the vagus nerve reports back to your brain what is going on in your organs. It is an essential part of the parasympathetic nervous system, which is responsible for calming organs after the stressed 'fight-or-flight' adrenaline response to danger.

Some people have stronger vagus tone, which means their bodies can relax faster after stress, making them less prone to inflammation-related disease. Research shows that a high vagal tone makes your body better at regulating blood glucose levels, reducing the likelihood of diabetes, stroke and cardiovascular disease. Low vagal tone, however, has been associated with chronic inflammation and painful related conditions like rheumatoid arthritis. There are attempts to improve vagal tone electrically, but it is already known that non-invasive, consciousness-based methods are effective.

Mindfulness Increases Gray Matter

In a study of long-term practitioners, neuroscientists found that experienced meditators had more gray matter in the frontal cortex.

The frontal cortex is linked to decision-making and to working memory. Most cortices shrink as they age, but 50-year-old meditators in the study had a similar amount of gray matter as 25 year olds.

In a second study, the team led by Sara Lazar of Mass General and Harvard Medical School observed people with no experience in an eight-week program of mindfulness. Participants meditated for an average of 27 minutes per day. Previous studies suggest that significant results can be achieved by meditating for 15 to 20 minutes per day.

The researchers observed thickening in various regions of the brain, including the left hippocampus (involved in learning, memory, and emotional regulation); the temporoparietal junction (involved in empathy and the ability to have multiple perspectives); and a part of the brain stem called the bridge (where regulatory neurotransmitters are generated).

There was also the shrinkage of the amygdala, a region of the brain associated with fear, anxiety, and aggression. This reduction in amygdala size correlated with reduced levels of stress in these participants.

The reduction in stress can contribute not only to a better quality of life but also can prevent chronic diseases and decrease feelings of pain due to the reduction of inflammation. In addition to reducing health costs, they can reduce the doses of addictive opioids and other medication. Improved decision-making and creative ability as well as empathy with clients and coworkers are desirable in the new economy. Finally, meditative experiences can transform perspectives to solve personal challenges and even reveal new paradigms for improved coexistence at work, at home, in the community, and on the Planet.

You can work with Neuma Being coaches and consultants, an ecosystem community of various areas of expertise including energy mindfulness, to integral wellness for yourself, your family, team or community.

14. The Promise and Peril of Tech

Altered states take time, but healthy altered states can help us move from being driven by anxiety, stress and fear, according to scientists who presented at Transformative Technology Conference in Silicon Valley, November 9-10, 2019. Can technology related to well-being and mindfulness help us feel less fearful, nervous, anxious, tired, and bored? Can technology help us be driven by healthy relationships and values (purpose) rather than alienate us? Several attendees remarked that the emerging technology that was discussed at this conference has the potential to liberate or imprison the minds of the future. It all depends on having discussions of the ethical implications and standards before the technologies proliferate into an unsuspecting society.

Are you ready for wireless encephalograms (EEG) that can detect if an air traffic controller is sleepy (or if a worker is distracted)? Ultrasonic, light and electrical modulation of attention, learning, and mood can alleviate symptoms of Parkinson's, enhance learning and meditation — could it be misused to manipulate and sedate people? Could virtual reality turn into an immersive opium of the masses? These technologies are already here. Are we prepared?

The End of the Poker Face

How much privacy can there be, if you can't hide your brain wave activity? If thermal, electrical and chemical sensors can reveal your feelings? As sensors and artificial intelligence computes big data, human bodies can become nodes in the Internet of Things. What will we give up in the name of convenience? Empathic technology that can recognize your mood and improve brain plasticity or learning with individual customization holds great promise, if it is within our control. If it is controlled by big corporations and totalitarian states, the story will be quite different. Devices that, in some ways, know more about us than we do are coming very soon. They will recognize when your brain is working harder by detecting pupil dilation. Chemical analysis of your breath will indicate muscle tension. Will our spaces be optimized for our choices or will our choices be affected even more by the environment? Corticoid sensor patches like those developed at Stanford University can detect our stress levels, while vagus nerve stimulation via the ear could alleviate it or make us more stress-resilient over time.

Further driving this point, Peter Freer has reportedly developed a remote EEG or a non-contact neuromonitor. In practice, this means that people can now measure brain waves up to 20 centimeters (8 inches) away from the brain – even without you knowing, since it requires no probes and wires. Will employers monitor their worker's level of attention and deduct their pay when they are not performing at a high level? Could it prevent transportation sector accidents by monitoring the attention or alertness level of tired or distracted workers? Will workers and drivers be completely replaced by technology, meaning that simple versions of EEG can simply become more accessible and pervasive to improve the human experience? Only time will tell.

Cardio-Neurofeedback and AI

Deborah Rozman of the HeartMath Institute discussed heart-rate variability as a measure of well-being and raised the possibility that one person can "lift" the well-being of a group through a sort of resonant influence and coherent synchronization of heart electromagnetic fields. Attendees were able to "meet" Sofia, the artificial intelligence (AI) robot by Hanson Robotics, which was recently granted "citizenship" by Saudi Arabia. There was a talk by SingularityNET Foundation advocating for the de-centralization of AI to prevent it from being controlled by any one party. There were interesting demos of how tech like Sofia can recognize facial expressions and even guide meditation.

The Wandering Nerve

There were several scientific presentations on stimulation (for enhancing or blocking aspects of brain function). These included vagus nerve stimulation (VNS) by startups like Bodhi NeuroTech and eQuillity. Pulse generators treat epilepsy, with 33% odds of 50% or greater reduction of epileptic episodes. VNS, in one study, reduced body fat in pigs, and recovered 75% of cortex brain cells affected by a stroke in rats. It was also noted that experience plus stimulus achieved greater neuroplasticity or improved ability to learn and change behavior.

Effects were noticeable for depression. Rather than using invasive and expensive procedures, it is now possible to achieve stimulation through the ear (auricular branch of the vagus nerve). VNS decreases heart rate, increases HRV heart rate variability, increases perceived feelings of calm, and facilitates teaching of critical skills – in one study, it helped rehabilitate premature babies learning how to feed).
When paired with behavioral intervention or meditative practices, it appeared to enhance the experience (see – "supercharge your zen" article on tech-assisted meditation).

Ultrasound, Light and Electrical Stimulation

Jay Sanguineti of Alchemas described how ultrasound-based stimulation allows us to reach deeper areas of the brain. By reaching the default mode network, there can be decreased activation in self-referencial activity. This approach can quiet posterior cingulate cortex (PCC) with less chatter and sense of oneness with the environment. Dr. Sanjay Manchanda of the University of New Mexico demonstrated how one can achieve higher states of consciousness with low-level energy transfer to the brain. Near-infrared light appears to be even more effective at repairing, restoring and enhancing the brain.

One product, the Vielight, uses 600-1000 nm infrared LEDs with pulses of 10 and 40 Hz. Neurogamma has been used at 40 Hz to relieve symptoms of PTSD and cognitive decline, improve learning, and improve communication between brain regions (increase in gamma brain waves at rest and during mediation). An experimental unit aimed to stimulate gamma brain waves using multiple of 40 Hz (harmonics) between 40 and 200 Hz with exciting results, especially among experienced meditators. People reported less mental chatter, greater calm, sense of presence and connection.

Remote Patient Monitoring

Until recently, it was difficult for doctors in the US to prescribe transformative tech systems. Changes in US law now aim to facilitate Remote Patient Monitoring, by providing billable codes for Medicare insurance reimbursement. One company that will benefit from this development is Spire, known for the Pebble breathing monitor pendant which has been available at Apple Stores. It measures breathing and assesses stress and anxiety through a pendent. Now, Spire is releasing health tags to add to clothing (approximately $150/ea). They can run on a 2-year charge and can withstand washer and drier.

Is it possible to use the addictive nature of games from a mere money-making scheme to helping people? Some remorseful gaming creators are creating deceptively simple games paired with behavioral interventions to improve well-being. For example, the Uplift game features hot air balloons that get people to recognize words associated with positive emotional states.

Inside: The New Wild

Researcher Dr. Pablo Paredes joked that if you want to find a human, you should look for a chair. The Average American spends 60 minutes a day in car (90 minutes in the San Francisco Bay area). He presented his pervasive well-being lab to help turn indoor and in-vehicle spaces healthier. He also remarked that people forget, get bored and break stuff, so trans tech should be kept as simple as possible. What if your chair could detect stress and tension and nudge you to move and shift your mood? Could virtual reality be used to make long car rides less stressful and even alleviate motion sickness?

Many people are overworked, tired, angry, overweight, distracted, sad, unhappy, isolated (1:4 Americans suffers from some kind of psychological disorder). Stress management accounts for 60-80% of doctor visits, but only 3% get stress management treatment. The US is dealing with an epidemic opioid addiction. Part of the problem could be that humans did not evolve for the indoors – we could run from lions, but we cannot run from our boss or traffic jams. We spend 87% of time indoors and in vehicles ("the new wild" – see: robert sapolsky – why zebras don't get ulcers).

Many therapies or systems describe Efficacy (rates of successful completion). However, Efficiency (which accounts for attrition) is typically poor (less than 1%). In the future, we can keep people healthy with precision health through smarter, healthier environments (homes, offices and transportation) which do not require much active participation. Society could accomplish this through simple, subtle, engaging, non-obstructive sensors and subtle interventions.

Beyond VR & AR: Introducing IR, Internal Reality Tech

Increasingly, the economy and society of the future is shaped by creativity and empathy, both of which emerge from the human mind. Success in the future will belong to the curious and self-aware who succeed with creative problem solving and soft skills like empathetic interaction. How might we enhance the human psyche to improve well-being and performance (from learning and ideation to productivity)?

Transformative technologies (Trans Tech) complement the rise of virtual reality, augmented reality and mixed reality with a sort of internal reality (IR). In other words, there is a rich inner life that can be a sort of vitality, creative insight, empathy. Periodically, we see a new study demonstrating how mindful and other transformative mental states (like lucid dreaming) provide relief from symptoms of pain, anxiety, stress, and depression. What if technology could be leveraged to facilitate such states to enhance cognitive and emotional abilities and help us all express our fullest potential -- to express our "better selves?"

Trans Tech can help us amplify our empathy, collaboration, awareness, intuition, understanding, emotional self-regulation, and meaning-making. Trans Tech may help us deal with low engagement, loneliness, anxiety, stress, depression, pain, suicide, distraction, frustration, fatigue, and poor soft skills.

Objectively, these benefits translate into fewer sick days, greater motivation and productivity, less toxic workplaces, improved problem solving and decision-making, improved customer service and engagement. Internally, emotional wellness is the ability to successfully handle stress and adapt to change and difficult times - at home and at work.

Emotional wellness implies the ability to be aware of and accept our feelings, rather than deny them, have an optimistic approach to life, and enjoy life despite its occasional disappointments and frustrations. Enhanced well-being allows us to keep problems in perspective and bounce back from setbacks (resilience).

Trans Tech has the potential to enhance our performance, well-being, interactions, and to thrive at work, in school, in society, at home, and in our own inner life. The future of work, society, education will be shaped by our minds. If used ethically and responsibly, individuals will be able to use trans tech to contribute at an even higher level through an enhanced empathy, vitality, cognition and imagination.

Extended Reality (XR) is an umbrella term to encompass various ways in which technology is used to augment or transport our minds, including VR, AR, and MR. Virtual Reality (VR) typically involves a headset that can transport our mind into a computer- or video-generated environment. It can be so immersive that we temporarily lose track of our actual surroundings in objective space.

Augmented Reality (AR) overlays digital images over our vision, through projection, the video screen of smart devices, or a smart eyeglasses. Mixed Reality (MR) is an advanced type of AR whereby artificial intelligence is used to recognize aspects of the physical environment in view so that digital objects can react to them.

Nelson Abreu has coined the expressions Consciousness Reality (CR) and Internal Reality (IR) as other aspects of extended reality. Simply put, IR tech is meant to facilitate transformative, creative mental states. Rather than relying exclusively on computer-generated graphics, IR employs tech to stimulate our own minds to produce or shape neural "media" (visual, auditory, tactile and other experiences) from within. This type of technology uses the mind as a source of entertainment, relaxation, creative enhancement, well-being.

Tech can be used to either stimulate or modulate this "internal data," or our internal information can be used to affect our experience in some way. At its height, it holds the potential to facilitate important cognitive shifts and meaningful inspiration to make the world a better place. There may also be an overlap with other types of XR tech, such as when biological signals are used to interface with and affect technology or when VR is used to facilitate transformative states from within.

Neuma Being recently developed a digital art experience entitled Synaptic Projections, which crossed the boundaries between IR and AR. Participants are able to affect a digital artwork projected into the physical space with their mental activity. Specifically, the artwork responds to brainwave activity as measured by a Muse headband. The experience was debuted in Los Angeles' Chinatown on December 28, 2019 and a second edition will be presented on February 1, 2020.

The interactive art piece turned out to be a playful experience for individuals, who sought different ways to increase the predominance of measured gamma waves and then to hold them at a relatively high level as long as possible. Spontaneously, it became a game that involved others as they sought to either encourage, advise or even playfully distract the person wearing the EEG sensing headband. Synaptic Projections was also an educational experience as it peaked the curiosity of participants and spectators regarding neuroscience, mindfulness, and technology.

A clearer example of IR developed by Neuma Being is the Cymatix Recliner, which uses a proprietary system to control sound and vibration in specific patterns aimed to facilitate creative altered states and profound relaxation. In heightened or transformative mental states, especially with our eyes closed, our mental field can be entertained by images, sounds, and even sensations of movement projected into our awareness from within. Such creative and restful states can inspire and energize creative professionals. Finally, Neuma Being is also exploring how VR experiences can facilitate extraordinary and mindful states, which would overlap VR and IR.

Arguably, humans developed early technologies and techniques like the use of certain types of music to achieve special states of mind. The human body has built in "technology" to achieve mindful and altered states like lucid dreams, which can be used to simulate various scenarios and aide in problem solving and development of certain skills. Mindfulness practices themselves can be viewed as a type of IR that can help reach states of mind that can assist with reduction of stress, pain, and anxiety. At Neuma Being, we believe that design and technology can act as an aide - rather than a crutch or substitute - to our own innate abilities. IR tech can make transformative states more easily accessible to the masses and even support more experienced individuals through challenging moments.

The Tao of the Dow

15. The Commons in the World to Come

By Alfredo Cunhal Sendim

Three months ago, Lisbon bus stops proclaimed "The No-Limit Generation", through an advertising campaign for a media network. Now, let's think together, as Agostinho da Silva said: without limits on a finite planet already shaking and with 8 billion people like us, it is expected that this will not go well. The matter is simple. Who sets the limits of whom? But before we get lost there, why don't we think about our limits first, and try to organize ourselves into "communities" that transform parts of what "is everyone's and no one's", so that the result benefits those who participate?

Why not even the scale to guarantee sovereignty by creating a real alternative to the human dichotomy (because it does not seem to exist in the natural system) of States / Corporations, fleeing the formula of nationalism? Why don't we organize to manage our ecosystems, biodiversity, health, food, education, culture, gastronomy, folklore, information, technology, currency, and life? We should leave to the State only complementary activities of general regulation, justice and security, and national and international dialogue.

In fact, we have always done it and we continue to try to do it, despite the fact that empires appeared as almost the only solution to the scarcity we were creating. There it is, we convinced a few that there are no limits and we see the result.

And the problem, of course, is our limits, and those of others. So we created two types of people. Those who dedicate themselves to finding arguments to be able to live at the expense of the work of others, and those who work subjugated so that the former exist. The state, now reborn from the ashes, is surely too distant to establish the confidence necessary to make the leap to that new empire. Trust is lost from generation to generation: trust in ourselves, in others, in organizations, in the state, in those "responsible".

We have to turn the corner because what can we expect from a community, or social being without trust? (A psychologist, hahaha). How easy will it be to rebuild trust, near or far? Trust, of course, still exists and not just in a last flame in a lost cave. Despite the blockade of centralized states, trust continues to grow across the globe through communities of citizens, the Commons. These communities are real, virtual, inspired by multiple worldviews, beliefs, and insights; they form a colorful mosaic filled with realities.

CSA's/AMAP's (community supported agriculture), transition movements, eco-communities, community workshops, educational communities, cultural communities, integral cooperatives, mutual health, insurance, credit, housing, time banks, mutual help and assistance... This Covid-19 will help us to understand the clear difference of being in a reality that is self-governing or commanded by third parties. But it can also easily lead us to the formula "whoever puts things in order, the rest doesn't matter" and then we wake up governed by a Bolsonaro or Trump.

In fact, so far, it hasn't been like that. We and the rest of the people, instead of going out and breaking everything, have built more Commons, which encourage all those who find a way to get out of this story once and for all, to count the number of empires as if we were playing Russian roulette.

What then are the Commons?

The common goods themselves are the planet, the socio-cultural-environmental heritage, the body, the urban, the digital... The Commons are the management of these goods by self-governing communities, creating procedures and rules that guarantee the enjoyment and use amongst all, and prevent the appropriation of the good by just a few. They are a governance model operated by a network of cooperators, their communities and the planet. They are also a political process that calls us to act beyond the stratified forms of the market's externalities and the modern state.

It is also an economic alternative that produces reciprocity (gift), generosity and solidarity within communities (local or global), which place use value above exchange value. It is collective life - this collective being formed by humans, their creations, and the other living beings that co-inhabit the Earth (itself a living being). In other words, they are a socio-ecological system and are a cultural transformation of great proportions, as a result of a process based on affections, senses and spirituality. The Commons are a practical path to a life of joy and imagination.

In the Commons the focus is on what we need and create, not what we can sell; the result is abundance and not scarcity. Governance is polycentric, sociocratic and meritocratic; not being defined by the State/Market, social relations and power are decentralized, access to material resources is defined by limits and rules chosen by users, and access to non-material resources is open.
The result is a regeneration of the planet and emancipation and social inclusion. This is also called Silvopasture or Agroecology. It is also called Service. It is no longer what to maintain for millennia, for example, in the community management of the town of Lameiros.

Universal Basic Income hasn't replaced Unemployment Benefit and we haven't trained people to organize instead of collaborating with lower speculation human work. The Commons concern, as Marta Wengorovius always reminds us, is the One to the Two and to the Many. Perhaps there is confidence in us and in relation to one another with regards to the possibility of working with Many Commons.

Last September, the interesting book Free, Fair and Alive by David Bollier and Silke Helfrich and the movement The Insurgent Power of the Commons also appeared. Professor Antonio Lafuente, a Spanish friend of our teacher Ana LuÃsa Janeira, also developed remarkable work in the Ibero-American community.

Why are we not able to govern ourselves in smaller "states", instead of waiting for them to govern us well so that each one of us can continue to make a living? And how about the multinationals, left-wing commentator Daniel Olivera will ask? We have the potential to run out of funds easily because it is our alienated behavior that allows the theft of speculation.

After COVID-19, perhaps, now we understand that the value of wearing a mask is not the current exchange value. The current value is a hypocritical theft based on what we call the market and which allows us all to practice it daily. Why not make the mask?

To move forward it is obvious that we have to create a global legal regulation organization and a similar one for justice and planetary defense. Paulo Magalhães is already dealing with that through the project Common Home of Humanity, and well.

I end, again, with Agostinho da Silva, who, thinking of "the world to come", "that we will not call empire", wrote about our great vision, referring to Father António Vieira. "Since, for any impossibility, he did not explain how all of this would come, his Fifth Empire, how there would be economic equality, how instruction and education would be done, how it would become obsolete to command and obey, how to design, if possible, a general thinking that encompassed ideologies, philosophies or theologies of the various communities, not only those of the instigators, but also of those who adhered to us, today, if able, he has given us the task."

Nor the Preacher nor the Teacher told us how, but they left us clues. And all of them at this point, point to the Commons.

We will be able to do it, yes. .

Only we can be Saint Sebastian.

* * * * *

Alfredo Cunhal Sendim is the coordinator of the user and worker-owned cooperative known as the User Cooperative of Freixo do Meio. Freixo do Meio is so much more than a farm. It is a vital experiment in cooperative living, in decision-making, in restoring eco-systems and hope for resilience in a climate-challenged world. This modest agricultural engineer and philosopher-farmer attracts other co-creators of a better tomorrow into conversation and cooperation in this Alentejo farm that houses an incredible example of agro-ecology.

Born in Porto, Alfredo Cunhal Sendim spent his childhood in Lisbon, the city, Montemor-o-Novo, the countryside, and Ferragudo, the sea. He was 8 years old when the '74 Revolution led to his family's property being occupied and he was taken to finish primary school in Pamplona, the mountains, in Franco's Spain. He witnessed a second transition to democracy, diving into a culture very distinct from his own. He later returned with his family to Lisbon and Ferragudo, the city and the sea - the countryside would be postponed another 15 years. He completed high school and strengthened his relationship with the ocean through multiple forms of fishing. His attempt to study veterinary medicine took him to Évora and the Alentejo for 5 years. While he was studying zootechnics, he started helping his mother who had regained ownership of a few lands in the region.

In 1990, he moved to Freixo do Meio where step-by-step he has been developing a structuring social and agronomical project. He returned to Spain for three years where he studied rural economy. He taught at Évora University where he is still a member of the Superior Council of the University. In this period, he participated actively in the agronomical associative movement of the Alentejo region.

His search for the use of the land as a "Common Good" comes from a profound reflection on the exercise of ownership and the interaction models with the community and with nature during his 30-year practice as a farmer at Herdade do Freixo do Meio. Besides land management, he was an administrator of companies in the agro-food and cork sectors. He is a pioneer of national movements of Agroecology, Organic Farming, Permaculture, Agroforests and Food Sovereignty.

Awarded and recognized by the Iberian environmental sector, Alfredo Cunhal Sendim has promoted and represented these causes at distinct channels such as the National Ministry of Agriculture, the EU, FAO and civil society. More recently, he is one of the faces of the lawsuit "People for the Climate", represented by ten European families. He has two children.

Resource: Bio for Freixo do Meio:
https://www.herdadedofreixodomeio.pt/

16. Manifesto

I support the Conscious Leadership Manifesto! I, too, believe that a more conscious world is possible! I envision a world built upon dignity and respect for self and all life. I understand that environments that promote individual development of awareness, relationships, creativity and leadership lead to greater well-being.

Well-being, put simply, is what most people desire: health and happiness. However, science shows humans are, generally, not so great at finding happiness. The largest study on well-being reveals that strong relationships and a sense of purpose are among the strongest correlates of wellness and happiness. Organizations can promote well-being by providing authentic relationships, healthy habits, a sense of purpose, sufficient autonomy and opportunities for development or mastery.

I think that the world sorely lacks more conscious leaders - in businesses, in government, and in civil society - that can promote well-being at large. As such, I will seek to be a more conscious leader in my own way and to foster conscious leadership in others. I will encourage those in a position of influence to do the same.

I understand that when individuals are empowered to create and serve, they can enjoy offering the highest level of evolutionary accomplishment to society. I will do more and demand more as a relative, friend, neighbor, citizen, consumer, colleague, manager, educator, service provider, entrepreneur, public figure or community leader for more ethical and equitable humanity -- one that facilitates the realization of potential and promotes the richness of experiences and relationships.

I want a society that increasingly values the irreducible nature of our inner life and our collective synergies, including our desire to enjoy and share liberty, discovery, delight, inspiration, accomplishment, cooperation, and spiritual evolution.

Governments, schools and workplaces are responsible for helping every individual enjoy a more authentic and accomplished life. Individuals and teams in every community and organization can catalyze healthy changes at the deepest level of any process: our minds, our consciousness. I understand that changes at this root level, affect the basis of our relationships, attitudes, values, and patterns of behavior. Therefore, any effort and resource available to develop our consciousness should be studied and supported.

Each unhealthy, unhappy individual without opportunity for development is a loss for all human kind in all senses including ethically, economically, and culturally. I will join forces with all those who wish to develop a life, consciousness or development-centered civilization that brings out what makes you awe-some. Let us unleash untapped potential, innovation, will, attention, creativity, connection, beauty and vitality for individual liberty, social and ecological dignity and fraternal common good.

Please go to this link to sign a petition for prioritizing WELL-BEING and DEVELOPMENT for all!
http://tinyurl.com/clmanifesto

Afterword

Well-Being Economics, An Economy of Love

Paulo Vieira de Castro, best-selling Portuguese author and speaker on spirituality in organizations, interviewed Canadian economist Mark Anielski about economic progress and well-being.

Mark Anielski wrote the book *The Economics of Happiness* over 10 years ago. Later, in 2018, he authored *The Economy of Well-Being*. Paulo and Mark talked about the possibility of redefining the idea of economic progress based on well-being and happiness, and yet another civilizational justice. This means that the economy cannot be separated from the environmental, climatic and welfare commitment of all beings, too. Based on this certainty, it becomes very easy to realize that, especially today, there are very few economic decisions that, even from a strictly technical point of view, can be exclusively economic. Most of them will have to be sustainable, ethical and fair before that. Since that often does not happen, we find ourselves in an unprecedented planetary crisis.

Paulo: We are just enjoying the living conditions that the planet provides us. The same is true of all other sentient beings. Mark, how can we justify that economic indicators, as a rule, forget to measure civilizational well-being and happiness?

Mark: What I propose is an economy oriented toward well-being, based on the original definition of the word wealth which means "conditions of well-being", from 13th century etymology. Thus, all economic and monetary policy decisions must be oriented towards sustaining or improving the generalized conditions of well-being of a society as a whole, according to natural laws aligned with the fundamental values of a culture or society. The truth is that the economic model we have today is not genuine or authentic in the truest definition of economics and wealth. A well-being economy is concerned with the state of human beings in the context of a healthy or flourishing natural ecosystem. The laws of nature are the ethical basis of such an economy.

Paulo: We all know that the planet's resources are finite. The truth is that we already consume more natural resources than the planet can return to us. How can we support infinite economic growth? That's not possible...

Mark: The current (neoclassical) economic model is based on a narrow definition of wealth, that is, it boils down to financial capital or, so often, money. Note that money itself is a social invention. However, the main reason why the economy should continue to grow - as measured by a very limited measure of progress, namely GDP (gross domestic product) - is an increasing amount of unpayable monetary debts.

Now, we all know that money cannot buy love or happiness, yet we live as if the accumulation of that wealth was the key to our greatest dreams. So, despite the increase in economic prosperity over the past fifty years, there are many declining well-being conditions and happiness rates that have remained largely unchanged since the 1950s. Our metrics of economic progress do not reflect the values that make us happy. This is, for example, our supportive relationships, work with purpose, a prosperous environment and even our well-being, including the spiritual.

Paulo: Well-being means that people lead a balanced and meaningful life, committed to the happiness of a community. Especially if we take the issue of climate emergencies seriously, we urgently need to take alternative well-being measures. This is the time to do it or it will be too late. For that, we will have to explore more progressive economic and social alternatives, abandoning the development paradigm based exclusively on economic growth. Some countries are already taking the first steps in this direction. Scotland, Iceland, New Zealand, among others, are now presenting surprising proposals with a view to the common good, well-being and happiness. Alternative measures of genuine progress have been developed in several countries in recent years, moving away, for example, from the most requested indicator of economic growth (GDP). Can you tell us a little about this promising effort?

Mark: Measures of well-being and happiness have been evolving since the 2012 Bhutan Gross National Happiness (GNH) Congress, with annual publications since the first World Happiness Report by economists John Helliwell and Jeffrey Sachs. The World Happiness Report's measures on happiness and well-being have been applied in many countries and jurisdictions, including Canada. However, the full adoption of an economic model based on well-being by any nation, state or municipality has not yet been adopted. However, a recent sign of hope has emerged with the New Zealand welfare budget, dated May 2019. They were the first to formally incorporate well-being into the country's operating budget. The main focus of this budget appears to be on mental and emotional well-being, combating the rising rates of youth suicide and high levels of domestic violence.

Paulo: I believe that only through a society of common good, which contains within itself the emancipating principles of human democracy and economic democracy, will we reform policies. Thus, we will arrive at the Politics of the Commons, whose greatest challenge will be to guarantee the future of the planet. There can be no political democracy without economic democracy. In the absence of the latter, we run the risk of not being able to implement even a concept of economic justice. How can we relate democracy and well-being?

Mark: The way forward will be taken through some form of economic democracy in which there is a relationship and shared responsibilities among all members of society for the commitment to the well-being of others. I would call this the economy of love, where I would define love as the concern for the well-being of others. Love for me is an action, or verb, that requires moment-to-moment reflection on how my actions and choices affect my neighbor (the other) in a positive, neutral or negative way, as well as the rest of nature. This requires an examination of conscience. It also requires a commitment to our actions through the lens of virtue. Most societies and religions have established a set of virtues that, when examined accordingly, turn out to be similarities. However, societies have divorced from these virtues.

* * * * *

TOWARD A PLANETARY CONDO ASSOCIATION
by Paulo Vieira de Castro

The obligation to take care of our sister, Mother Earth [1] has been misunderstood since time immemorial. In such a way, attentive to my ideology, ecology, I announce another founding thought. There will be no social, economic, political, or any other justice, in the absence of environmental justice, since the world does not have an environmental or climate problem. This is the most common and dangerous of errors. The world has a problem that is, first and foremost, rooted in an irresponsible economic system. As long as we are not able to have the courage to change - progressively - the economic system, we will not be able to provide a complete solution to the environmental and climatic problems that affect all living beings, those born and not yet born, because in Nature everything is systemic. And why would life, the life between lives and the life after life not be? And, everything about us is that. We are, usually with the rest of Nature, the result of infinite ancestors. We are beings in transformation. The entire terrestrial system works in the same way. No exception.

Business dealings will have to prioritize human rights and the rights of the rest of Nature, imposing themselves on corporate rights.

Afterword

This means that the system must be fair and just before it is free. Here free is used in the way we know it from current practice.

So, we come to a handful of words for which we forget the spirit that was at their origin. For example, justice, democracy, ideology, Nature, economy, politics, ... Unfortunately, today we are left by the letter, the form and very little by the kindness that gave rise to them. Thus a new social grammar is born. And with it populism and fake news.

Another example, to better understand this question: What is the fair price for all trees in the Amazon? Now, anyone in the economic field will know how to give you a complete answer in this regard. The fair price is what the customer is willing to pay. But is it really that simple? Not...

The deforestation of this forest, or not, results from the principle of the sovereignty of the countries and, still, from the laws that protect the owners of the lands in which such trees grow freely. However, the oxygen that this forest produces is from all beings in nature. Thus it is understood, too, that trade cannot be free if it is not fair. And, this applies to any and all economic activity, especially if it involves sustainability issues. In a time of climatic emergency it will be easier to understand that our common home is priceless. The common must be taken care of by everyone, without exception. Hence understanding the idea of the Economy of Caring and the Economy of the Common.

But, let's go back to our example. It is not only trade that is not fair. When we think of our common home, we have been using a formula that measures impact by economically unfair benchmarks. I am referring particularly to the GDP.

Let's see. Let us imagine that the countries involved in deforestation in the Amazon cut down all the trees there and then sold them. What would happen? Economic growth, as measured by the flawed benchmark (gross domestic product), skyrocketed - on the positive side - to levels never reached in those countries. Despite this, life on the planet, as you will imagine, is forever compromised for all. People, animals and Nature will be closer to disappearing.

The proof that our common home was not considered a human right, is the disappearance in the last 50 years of thousands of species that have coexisted in it. In addition, there is a greater inequality between the most favored and the poorest strata. The appearance and growth of multiple diseases related to climatic and environmental issues, transposed to all species. How can we consider the current economic system just when we don't think of all people, all animals, in the context of Nature that is our common home?

For that reason I bring forth some concerns, ideas, and many doubts, in thinking about the progressive change of the economic system to Portugal. I hope that in the next 20 years our country, in its process of transformation towards an economic democracy, and based on environmental justice, will be considered a cluster of public/private organizations, profitable and non-profit related to these flags: Environmental Justice and Economic Democracy.

The Earth System

In this regard, I spoke with Paulo Magalhães. Ahead of his time, more than a decade ago he saw his book published: O CondomÃnio da Terra. From Climate Change to a New Legal Conception of the Planet [2] . More recently, with a multifaceted group of national and foreign experts, he created the association The Common House of Humanity [3] . This association's conceptual roots are sought in this founding book, with the intention of developing a global governance model for the earth's natural resources. It takes account of the economies of all countries based on at least 9 scientific indicators in defense of the common good that is, after all, the home of all of us. The common good is thus defined as the Earth System itself - the system that supports life on our planet - and which should be recognized as an intangible heritage of humanity.

Environmental justice

Afterword

When it comes to legally administering a planet, Magalhaes is part of a very simple idea: an Earth System with a view to maintaining the common in a favorable way to all beings. He designed a legal support for global governance that looks at the planet not as a territory but as a system, thus moving away from the common conception of international law that only sees the planet as a territory and its borders. He warns us of the following: First, develop a model to measure and manage the global impacts that each country has on the Earth System. It is, therefore, a mode of governance on a global scale that allows us to define the common good. Second, list the activities that are beneficial and those that are not, creating rules of congruence between the provision of the good and the use of it. Third, create a (global) administration system of that very good - The Earth System, which is impossible to divide, even if in a legally abstract way.

In addition to the territory, there is a common good that exists inside and outside all borders, the Functional System that supports life, and that today is scientifically possible to define and delimit. Note that for the current Law there are no legal assets that exist inside and outside the sovereignties imposed by the borders. What Magalhaes proposes will be the first global legal asset.

Science and environment

Magalhaes continues to explain in an uncomplicated way that in scientific terms, our common home is not the planet, because during most of its existence conditions were not created for sentient life to exist here. Today, too, the planet is partly out of favor, that is, it's not the ideal biogeophysical structure for human life and that of other beings. Scientists have defined a safe space for humanity. This is the result of 9 indicators, with maximum and minimum admissible values, which make it possible to identify the biogeophysical structure of the Holocene, that is, from the last 11,000 years. Our common home is this: a state favorable to human life and that of all beings. It is not the planet, because this, the planet, was not always favorable to life as we know it.

The economic view

For him, for example, the wealth of the Amazon cannot be simply measured in square kilometers, or in tons of wood, meat or soy. Its wealth must be found according to the total amount of biochemical functions and physical processes it provides to the Earth System.

The climate emergency calls us to a paradigm shift, he argues. Countries that have sovereignty over the Amazon can only incorporate economic value through the GDP. In other words, chopping wood, selling cattle or planting soy, ..., because the biophysical, intangible work of the Amazon is not recognized as an indicator of economic growth. However, a sustainable economy will only be possible if it is able to ensure the maintenance of the system. That is, capable of maintaining biogeophysical conditions. In conclusion, keeping the Earth System in good working order has to be an economic activity. And that is not what is happening today, because this "biogeophysical work of nature" is not recognized by law, and is also invisible to the economy.

In order to make this possible, the countries that contribute to the essential maintenance of the Earth System must have income from there. Nature's work has to be turned into economic activity. It is enough to account for what each country does positive and negative to the Earth System.

Magalhaes leads us to understand the nuances of economic reality in the face of environmental issues, alerting us to the need to connect economic cycles with natural cycles, proposing a financial contribution in exchange for the invisible work of Nature. Without an economy of natural intangibles, we will never be sustainable, he says. This is because any system, whatever it is, needs maintenance.

Afterword

The Terrestrial Condominium

For Paulo Magalhaes, mixing private interests with the maintenance of the common good, existing inside and outside all borders, meets a management model already present in our daily lives: the condominium of our homes. That is, the overlapping of two legal regimes within the same space, ensuring the maintenance of the common good without losing the private dimension. For the administration of the terrestrial condominium he proposes the global governance of the United Nations, through the Trusteeship Council, that is, the Guardianship Council of the United Nations. This would be in charge of maintaining the ecosystem by agreeing economists, scientists, jurists, among others.

Nature and women

What do nature and women have in common? It is that both do an essential job that many insist on continuing to ignore. It's called caring. For this reason, this month's article is about the need to alert to the way women and mother nature are subjugated by a model of economic development that contributes to deepening inequalities, invisibility, increasing ecological deterioration, exposing, still, the biophysical limits of the Earth. However, their fate, women and nature, is closely linked to the future of the planet, so words like ecology, eco-feminism and eco-justice are now inseparable.
Invisible work: As a rule, women add more hours to their working hours than men in unpaid terms. Examples of this are household chores and caregiving. Thus activities dedicated to the well-being of families and communities are so often ignored by economic indicators. This is called an invisible economy because it is not remunerated, making it, therefore, impossible to be reflected as an effort to create wealth for a country. At least through the most common indicator: GDP. It should be noted that in the case of women,

the international community even made this commitment in the 2030 Agenda for Sustainable Development.

To give you an idea, in 2017 , unpaid domestic work such as cooking, cleaning the house, taking care of children and the elderly, most often done by women, could have represented between 10% to 39% of the countries' Gross Domestic Product (GDP). This was according to UN Women. Likewise, in the book The invisible side of the economy, Swedish Katrine Marçal says, "if we want a complete picture of the economy, we cannot ignore what half the population does during half the time". The author reveals data like that of Canada's national statistics agency, predicting that the value of unpaid work [4] in the country ranged from 30.6 to 41.4% of GDP [5] .

Invisible environment: In the same way as women, nature is devalued due to the failure to recognize the harm we do to it. This is particularly so through unfair economic models. Let's do the same simple exercise. What is the fair price for all trees in the Amazon rainforest? It is priceless because the air it recycles is the property of all beings of nature.. Thus it is understood that the economy can only be free if it is not unfair. And, this applies to any and all human-sponsored activity.

In a time of climatic emergency, like the present, it will be easier to understand that our Common House is priceless. This, the common one, should be taken care of by everyone, without exception. Hence the idea of economic empathy and the economy of the common good that we have already spoken about here several times.

The method we use to measure economic growth is so often inept. As previously mentioned, if all the trees in the Amazon were cut and then sold, economic growth and wealth, measured by the flawed reference indicator (GDP - gross domestic product), would skyrocket - on the positive side - to levels never reached in those countries. Despite this, life on the planet, as you can imagine, would be forever compromised. All beings would be closer to their extinction. What wealth is this? The famous GDP, the indicator of a country's wealth, of which we have heard so much, does not consider the environmental impacts in its accounts. Incidentally J.F. Kennedy, the most mythical president of the USA, stated in 1968 in this respect: GDP measures everything but what is of interest.

How can we consider the current economic system free or fair when what we know about it is the price of everything and the value of nothing? It is therefore urgent to propose a progressive change in the economic system. This is in the hope that in the coming years a process of collaborative transformation for a truly sustainable economy of public, private, profitable and non-profit organizations can be launched. Starting from the simple to the complex, from local to global, from Nature to Nature, we need to be thinking about the economy based on the ecosystem. We are in pursuit of a greener, more blue and, above all, fairer economy.

To understand this, let us start with the most basic rules of economic justice. They will have to prioritize human rights and the rights of the rest, as compared to most corporate rights. Note that the economy needs to be socially regulated, while nature can, and should, exist with the minimum of any economic interference. The regulation of nature by the economy is largely responsible for the excessive environmental and climate crisis. As already mentioned here, we urgently need to adopt alternative measures of well-being for all without exception. If we don't, it may be too late. For that, we will have to explore more progressive economic and social alternatives, abandoning the development paradigm based exclusively on economic growth.

Based on this conviction, it becomes easy to see that, especially today, there are very few economic decisions that, even from a strictly technical point of view, can be exclusively economic. Most of them will have to be, above all, sustainable, ethical and moral. That is why it is not always the case that we find ourselves in an unprecedented planetary crisis, thus grounding ourselves on the conviction that the environment, the climate and the economy cannot be separated.

Conclusion? More than an environmental problem, the world has a problem that is, first of all, rooted in an exhausted economic system. As long as we are not able to have the courage to make alternative and complementary proposals to the current economic system, we will not be competent enough to one day provide a complete solution to the planet's social, environmental and climate problems.

Papalagui's destructive economy

I remembered reading a collection of texts before the first world war, how little human beings have evolved since then.
Excerpt from Erich Scheurmann's O Papalagui [6]. Branco, the Lord as he was called by the tender chief of the Tuiavii tribe of Tiavéa (the distant islet of Upolu, in Samoa, in the South Seas). An essential narrative for anyone who wants to understand the unconscious matrix of Western economies today.
Definitely, a useful vision for a better understanding of the current world .
But, what can we learn from Tuiavii, an individual still closely linked to Nature? He tells us how he sees us, as well as Western culture. In the introduction of the work, we discovered our own contemporary reality. How much we've already lost. Simplicity, authenticity, solidarity. The being that makes us human. All of that was left behind.
The chief of this primitive tribe is very clear in his intention to reveal the danger of Papalagui, the "enlightened peoples of the European continent", stating that "the worst mistake made by their ancestors was to believe that the light of Europe would bring them happiness". I speak of a chief who "lived in general as a child, only under the empire of the senses, entirely in the present and without becoming aware of himself or of what was near or far around him, ..." however "was aware of being, that inner force that above all distinguishes us from the primitive tribes ".
It is this yearning to know that takes him as an adult to tread European lands. In his wanderings through the land of Papalagui, Tuiavii marvels at the fact that everyone is obsessed with money. Referring to "greed, his gaze is fixed on everything that touches money". Strange, yet, that "not everyone who has a lot of money works a lot (They all would like to have a lot of money without

working)". Referring, still in this respect to Papalagui, that it is "thanks to this doctrine, fomented by money, that he allows himself to be cruel". In addition, "the rich man does not know if the honors they pay him are due to his person or his money; most of the time it is your money ". He parallels what happens in his tribe, where "they say that someone who demands something for the hospitality he offers is worthy of contempt ...". "... for every fruit you give!".

Tuiavii, the Aboriginal leader, wishes that the people of the Tiavéa people never become in their hearts "like Papalagui, who is able to feel happy and content even when, at his side, his brother is sad and unhappy". Ending by stating that "it is not possible to help anyone with money and make them really happier, stronger and happier ...", just for that. Also responsible for this disenchantment is, in his opinion, "the serious disease of always thinking". And today we know that it is so. Fernando Pessoa, through his heteronym Alberto Caeiro, said, in this respect, that "to think is to be sick of the eyes". Well, we will think less. And repair more. So I understand it.

Rehabilitate the real

Once we find ourselves in a time of climatic emergency, we have no time to discover a new way home. We will only be left with the possibility of rewriting a new ending to this story that I now tell you. We cannot go back to 1969. The North American visionary Buckminster Fuller, in his classic on ecological literature "Instruction Manual for the Spaceship Earth" referred to the wisdom that emanates more, exclusively, from erudite knowledge, from scientific knowledge, but an innocence from an almost divine source. It was this same conscience that motivated Tuiavii or Greta Thunberg. These are the essentials for this shift in consciousness.

Many years ago I realized that people who are crazy enough to think they can change the world are just the ones who do. Salvador Dali reiterated the importance of this madness that founded human evolution, "the only difference between me and a madman is that I am not mad". It is impossible to ignore an essential madman, as he is the one who inspires radical change, forcing us to evolve in various dimensions of our existence. There is a primary condition that ties them together: an immense belief. In fact, also for this reason, I believe that it was these same madmen who invented love.

To better understand it, we will have to recover founding concepts in an attempt to rehabilitate the real. For that we will have to do as Claude Monet taught us. Forget the name of things. Well, I believe that, in our times, only this will allow us not to become just those same things. In addition, we will have to dispense with words since, for me, this is the most cruel error of specialization of the human race. We can speak instead of what we think, feel or act. And this induces in us the illusion of being what we are not, saying what we don't practice, ..., getting entangled with the accessory at the expense of the essential. That is how we came to humanity's greatest mistake.

The reality is that we are just users of this planet. We are not the owners of their lands, their people, their flora, etc. In addition, we came into the world empty-handed, ending the breath we call life in the same way, empty-handed. What to do? Change the starting point, because the logic that brought us here, will not be the one that will get us out of here. I insist.

That is how we lost our values, feelings, and emotions. And so we lose track of reality, this very permanent illusion, as Einstein well defined it. Fundamentally, the truth is that reality does not need us. If you understand things, they are exactly what they are. If you don't understand things, they are exactly what they are.

We lack a starting point. We only share dreams and destinations. We, too, are this: the origin. We've been too concerned about where we're going. Thus, so often, the confusion between message and messenger is justified. Between lighting and light source. We should also keep in mind that the planet concentrates a common vibration in itself, that which connects us all to the original harmony, privileging the connection with the ever-present source.

Living and dying will be no more than a return home, return to the origin. The whole existence is a space of change, evolution and human transformation. Hence the emergence of a radical compromise.

How do I explain this to the most rational minds? By increasing our knowledge about the alchemy of origin, I remember that everything at the origin is immaterial. On the other hand, intelligence, despite proving to be essential, because reason avoids error, brought us duality, conditioning intuitive nature. So, we stopped living in Nature. The limitations imposed on the intuitive took us away from ourselves, frightening us. That is why there is so much suffering and fear in contemporary society.

* * * * *

[1] In 2015 Pope Francis came to the defense of the planet in his Encyclical Our Common House.
[2] Editora Almedina (2007).
[3] This association has its headquarters at the University of Porto. Infos: https://www.commonhomeofhumanity.org/
[4] Designed.
[5] Depending on the measurement method.
[6] Erich Scheurmann, O Papalagui - speeches by Tuiavii Chief of tribe of Tiavéa in the South Seas, Editora AntÃgona, Lisbon. 10th edition.

The Tao of the Dow

About the Author

All rights reserved NEUMASCAPE STUDIO, Inc.
Photo by Emi Kitawaki and Jen Whittaker

Nelson Correia Abreu, BSEE, PE, MS is a registered electrical engineer, specializing in smart grids, with a Masters in Design, Business and Technology in Los Angeles. He is an entrepreneur, inventor, author and educator. A descendent of Goa, India, he was born and raised in Lisbon, Portugal.

For years, Nelson has been exploring the intersection of being, society and technology: how extraordinary states facilitate new technical and social solutions (innovation) and how technology can facilitate such states. He is the CTO and co-founder of Neumascape Studio and Neuma Being. He is a member of the ICRL consortium (formerly Princeton Engineering Anomalies Research lab); he has served as Assistant Scientific Director for non-profit International Academy of Consciousness and Student Member Representative of the Society for Scientific Exploration board.

He has lectured to lay and academic audiences for 20 years in five continents and developed novel technologies and techniques to induce states of awareness, creativity, safety and well-being, holding two patent filings. Nelson continues to develop novel ways to reduce stress, anxiety, and pain and to improve creativity, performance, self-knowledge and intuition. He has contributed to several publications and co-authored "Ordinary People, Extraordinary Experiences."

He has pioneered the development of transformative technologies for industrial safety: innovations that can save lives. Beside coining CR and IR tech (consciousness reality or internal reality tech), he has contributed to the development of conscious leadership. Nelson has also championed numerous process improvements for the electrical industry that have created millions of dollars of value.

Through creative leadership, innovative process changes and new tools and methods, he has contributed to a smarter, safer, more reliable and greener electrical power grid: from transmission stations in California to wind farms in Iowa to solar farms in Puerto Rico.

You can read more from Nelson Abreu in the following books:

Co-authored:
Ordinary People, Extraordinary Experiences, November 2018, Consciousness Publishing

Contributed Chapters:
Being and Biology: Is Consciousness the Life Force?, edited by Brenda Dunne & Robert Jahn (ICRL Press, 2017)

Consciousness Beyond the Body, edited by Alexander de Foe (Melbourne Centre for Exceptional Human Potential, 2016)

Out-of-Body Experiences: An Experiential Anthology, edited by Rodrigo Montenegro (International Academy of Consciousness, 2015)

Filters and Reflections: Perspectives on Reality, edited by Zachary Jones et al, (ICRL Press, 2009)

About the Author

Journal Publications:
Journal on Consciousness, various issues

http://www.sintropia.it/journal/english/2013-eng-2-0-index.pdf

https://books.google.com/books?id=M-YzBwAAQBAJ&pg=PA39&lpg=PA39&dq=autoricerca+nelson+abreu&source=bl&ots=5zoM5cX2Xi&sig=oi_TUBM-RMxecMMBZ6gusAgaC5Q&hl=en&sa=X&ei=I7c_VdqTENL5yQTjtIHIAg&ved=0CCAQ6AEwAA#v=onepage&q=autoricerca%20nelson%20abreu&f=false

The Tao of the Dow

Praise for The Tao of the Dow

More than a transformative legacy, this book contains, in itself, a seed of profound goodness. N. Abreu presents us with an inspiring vision, doing so through the sharing of countless and so necessary alternative possibilities for a way forward. Definitely, a must-read book.
-Paulo Vieira de Castro, MSc (Portugal), Author of The Book of Pain and Suffering (2019)

Nelson Abreu's new book breaks new ground on how we have a golden opportunity to reset our economic models to ones rooted in loving and attentive presence. Nelson directly addresses the exclusive bias of the present economic growth paradigm based on greed, and provides a transformative approach using the latest research from consciousness studies. The NEUMA innovation team are building a cooperative and sustainable system promoting well-being, and benefitting all without class distinctions. A must read, even more so, a must is to experience NEUMA!
-Dr. C. M. Chantal Toporow, Education Chair, Society for Scientific Exploration

Nelson Abreu has produced a tour-de-force of ideas for a better life world, a better world. An extraordinary accomplishment - at a very important time. It should be read and discussed widely, starting in high schools.
-Dr. Torben Riise, biotech scientist, executive, author, speaker

The Tao of the Dow, *authored by Nelson Abreu is a clarion call to raise our individual and collective consciousness (awareness) that love is our essence. That well-being is our birth right. That our life is a path of love. Abreu, an engineer by profession, is one of those rare people who understands the science of consciousness and happiness. To*

develop consciousness entails a surrender to the wisdom of love and joy. Abreu knows that an economy based on well-being is possible to the extent that there is a sufficient level of conscious individuals who understand what nurtures our spirit and soul. Abreu understands like Aristotle that happiness means 'well-being of the soul/spirit' from the Greek word eudaimonia. As an economist specializing in well-being, Nelson Abreu shows us that technology and systems based on well-being are possible whether in our own lives, the lives of our family, our workplace and communities. High levels of consciousness entail an experience of joy and love, as per the earlier work of Dr. David R Hawkins (Power vs Force). The essence of Tao (or the Way) is the harmony of eight forms; the Way is the Path of Love. It is refreshing to read The Tao of the Dow and know that there is a practical system that we can co-create that helps build an economy based on well-being and a higher consciousness of love.
-Mark Anielski, author of *The Economics of Happiness* and *An Economy of Well-being*

I believe **The Tao of the Dow** *is the path to lead us to return to a golden age of conscience. It's a wonderful book. Without organizing ideas, it's difficult for coordinated action to happen for human dignity. The Tao of the Dow is a documented invitation to a new narrative - one that is a true light of hope, not only for goodness but also for possibility. The astonishment of the COVID moment opens many of us to participate in these ideas, so nicely laid out here. Thank you Nelson for your clear, honest, lucid, simple, deep, and open testimony, based on your research and experience. It provides evidence that we belong to the stars.*
-Alfredo Cunhal Sendim, renown agro-ecology expert

The economy is more than just management of money. It can (and it should) encompass the ethical management of the resources of other

Praise for *The Tao of the Dow*

beings like time, energy, ideas, creativity and life's opportunities — especially in the face of climate change, inequality and crises like COVID-19. Nelson Abreu goes beyond criticizing and theorizing by discussing feasible approaches and offers practical ways for optimizing evolution of human society, without costing either souls or our biosphere. I happen to be a close friend for more than 20 years, following Nelson's growth and work, which always aims to improve and enrich the lives of others and of society in general - The Tao of the Dow is no exception.
-Wagner Alegretti, BSEE, co-founder of International Academy of Consciousness, Institute of Applied Consciousness Technologies, author of *Retrocognitions*

www.ingramcontent.com/pod-product-compliance
Lightning Source LLC
Chambersburg PA
CBHW071359210526
45465CB00001B/172